CARDIOLOGY
AT THE LIMITS II

CARDIOLOGY
AT THE LIMITS II

edited by
Derek M Yellon
Lionel H Opie

Based on a symposium held in
Cape Town to celebrate the
ongoing collaboration between
University of Cape Town
and
University College London
in the form of the Roche Joint Chair
of Cellular Cardiology and the
Hatter Institutes of both Medical Schools

Authors' Publishing House,
New York.

Stanford Writers, Cape Town

University of Cape Town
and
University College London
1998

In no case can the institutions with which the authors are affiliated or the publisher be held responsible for the views expressed in the book, which reflect the opinions of the authors. Please call any errors to the attention of the authors.

ISBN: 0-620-23258-7

Cover, title and book copyright by Lionel Opie and Derek Yellon. The authors retain rights to their individual chapters.

Authors' Publishing House, Symposium Series

Printed in South Africa by
The Rustica Press, Ndabeni, Western Cape
D6466

Edited by
Derek M Yellon
Director of Institute and Head of Division of Cardiology
The Hatter Institute and Centre for Cardiology
University College Hospital and Medical School
London, United Kingdom

Lionel H Opie
Professor of Medicine and
Director, Heart Research Unit and Cape Heart Centre
University of Cape Town
Cape Town, South Africa

With prefaces by
Professor Wieland Gevers
Senior Deputy Vice-Chancellor
University of Cape Town
Cape Town, South Africa

Sir Derek Roberts, CBE, FRS, FEng
Provost
University College London
London, United Kingdom

Chapter

PRINCIPAL CONTRIBUTING AUTHORS

Professor Morris Brown, MA, MSc, MD, FRCP
Professor of Clinical Pharmacology
University of Cambridge
Addenbrookes Hospital
Cambridge, England

Professor Stuart M Cobbe, MD, PhD
Professor of Medical Cardiology
Royal Infirmary
Glasgow, Scotland

Professor Salvador E Moncada, FRCP, FRS
Professor of Experimental Biology & Therapeutics
Director of the Cruciform Project
University College London
England

Professor Denis Noble, PhD, FRS, Hon FRCP
Burdon Sanderson Professor of Cardiovascular Physiology
University of Oxford
Oxford, England

Professor Thomas A Pearson, MD, PhD
Albert D Kaiser Professor and Chair
University of Rochester School of Medicine
Rochester
New York, USA

Dr Michael N Sack, MS, MD
Senior Lecturer and Director of the Hatter Institute
Cape Town
University College Hospital and Medical School
London, England

Professor Frans J van de Werf, MD, FESC
Professor of Medicine
University Hospital Gasthuisberg
Leuven, Belgium

Professor Hugh Watkins, MD, PhD, FRCP
Professor of Cardiovascular Medicine
John Radcliffe Hospital
Oxford, England

PREFACE FROM THE SENIOR DEPUTY VICE-CHANCELLOR, UNIVERSITY OF CAPE TOWN

"Cardiology at the Limits", the title of this book and the Conference from which it has sprung, refers to the exploration of new and technically sophisticated concepts by leading authorities on the heart and its machinations. The opening session in the BMW Imax Cinema Hall took its audience symbolically to the limits of slide projection for a masterly review paper. Other papers that followed were visually less spectacular but just as bold and interesting. The collaboration between the linked research groups, one at University College London and the other at the University of Cape Town, continues to gain momentum; it allows us to develop the knowledge and deep insights that will be necessary to provide better health care to large populations of people sorely in need of it. Primary health care can only work if it is based on the capacity to turn a real scientific understanding of subjects such as the heart and circulation into health delivery at the times and in the places where it matters.

UCT is fortunate in its involvement in this enterprise, in the people who started and inspired them, and in those who take part in it. The continued generosity of Roche Pharmaceuticals in supporting this is gratefully acknowledged, as is that of Mr Maurice Hatter.

Professor Wieland Gevers

PREFACE FROM THE PROVOST, UNIVERSITY COLLEGE, LONDON

All successful research starts with the identification of a significant problem. What makes bio-medical research special is that after that first step it is also necessary to create a number of essential partnerships between:

- Research, education and training
- Basic and clinical research
- Academic research and the delivery of healthcare
- Academe and industry – typified by Roche's sponsorship of this meeting and of Michael Sack's post as first Director of the Hatter Institute for Cardiovascular Studies at the University of Cape Town (UCT).

The two Hatter Institutes, at UCL and UCT, recognise the above imperatives. They also recognise the importance of international collaboration. This is why this is another milestone on our progress to the Limits of Cardiology.

Sir Derek Roberts, CBE, FRS, FEng

We are privileged to present this, the second in the series on Cardiology at the Limits.

The extraordinary rate at which cardiovascular research continues to progress, to the ultimate benefit of our patients, is as impressive now as it was last year when we started our series on Cardiology at the Limits. As before, the book is based on a workshop held in Cape Town, organized jointly by both of us under the aegis of our respective Universities, and with the active interaction between the Hatter Institute of University College London, and the Hatter Institute, University of Cape Town. The opening was attended by both Sir Derek Roberts, the Provost of University College London, and Professor W Gevers, Senior Deputy Vice-Chancellor, University of Cape Town. Both have sent warm messages of goodwill for the success of this book. As before, Roche pharmaceuticals have come to the support of this novel venture, and we thank them warmly for their continued efforts to promote knowledge that is at the cutting edge of cardiovascular advance.

On this occasion, the subjects high-lighted in the various chapters differ in nature from our first "At the Limits" meeting. Then we varied from the effects of poverty and affluence on cardiovascular disease, to acute interventions such as thrombolytic therapy and primary angioplasty for acute myocardial infarction. On this occasion, we start with cardiovascular diseases in developing countries and go on to the blood vessels, with current information on cholesterol, platelets, anti-oxidants, and nitric oxide. There is a new emphasis on molecular biology of cardiomyopathy, left ventricular hypertrophy and the failing left ventricle. Electrophysiology concentrates on the role of T and L type calcium channels. These outstanding papers by leading experts carry forward the fine tradition initiated by the first series on Cardiology at the Limits.

We plan to continue this series of meetings and publications, with the aim of covering the major advances that place cardiology at the limits of the advance of medical science.

Lionel H. Opie
Derek M. Yellon

CHAPTER 1

Cardiovascular Disease in Developing Countries:

Myths, Realities, and Opportunities

Thomas A. Pearson

INTRODUCTION

Cardiovascular diseases (CVD), especially those related to atherosclerosis and hypertension, have traditionally been considered diseases of Occidental societies, namely Western Europe, North America, and Australia/New Zealand. For the remainder of the world, especially those countries with less economic development, the major health concerns have been focused on infectious, parasitic, nutritional, and perinatal diseases. While this "unfinished agenda" has by no means disappeared, the major thesis of this paper is that an epidemic of heart disease and stroke may be inevitable for the developing world in lieu of early action, and the only hope to blunt its impact is to understand its origins, predict its magnitude, and organize preventive and case management resources prior to its establishment.

To develop this thesis, this manuscript will first describe the impact of the so-called "epidemiologic transition" on cardiovascular disease, describing the various phases that countries and cultures might pass through. With this somewhat theoretical background, cardiovascular disease in various regions of the world, including Sub Saharan Africa, will be described for the 1990s, dispelling a number of myths about CVD as currently observed in the developing world. Next, projections to the year 2020 will estimate the continued expansion of this epidemic as well as its causes. The possibility that the current worrisome projections in fact underestimate the future magnitude of the problem will be supported by discussion of several other factors which might potentiate the risk of CVD in developing countries. Finally, strategies for prevention and case management will be reviewed, identifying opportunities for research and development which are currently being initiated by a small number of interested organizations.

THE DYNAMIC NATURE OF PATTERNS OF CARDIOVASCULAR DISEASE

There is the tendency to assume that a population's current patterns of morbidity and mortality have existed for some time and will continue to define a population's health. As far as cardiovascular disease is concerned, this is far from the truth, with dynamic trends in mortality noted between and within countries. To try to understand and even predict these trends, the concept of the so-called "epidemiologic transition" is useful. The epidemiologic transition occurs when basic human needs for water, food, shelter, and medical care reduce the burden of infectious, parasitic, nutritional, and perinatal diseases to the point where life expectancy rises above 50 to 55 years (1,2). At this point, the number of deaths from cardiovascular disease exceed those from infectious and parasitic diseases, and the population disease pattern has transitioned to one dominated by chronic diseases.

Rather than view the epidemiologic transition as a discrete event, it might be considered to be an evolutionary process, with at least four phases proposed (1,3) (Table 1-1). Cardiovascular disease has played a role in every phase of the epidemiologic transition, including the first phase (that of pestilence and famine), in which rheumatic heart disease and inflammatory cardiomyopathies (e.g. viral myocarditis, Chagas disease, beri-beri heart disease, etc.) account for a small proportion of deaths. Isolated areas of several regions, including Sub Saharan Africa, South America, and India, remain in this phase (Table 1-2). However, the contention is

TABLE 1-1. CARDIOVASCULAR DISEASES AT DIFFERING PHASES IN THE EPIDEMIOLOGIC TRANSITION IN 1990.

Phase of Epidemiologic Transition	Deaths from CVD (%)	Predominant Cardiovascular Diseases	Regional Examples in 1990
Age of pestilence and famine	5-10	Rheumatic heart disease Infections and nutritional cardio-myopathies	Sub Saharan Africa, Rural India, and South America
Age of receding pandemics	10-35	As above, plus hypertensive heart disease and hemorrhagic stroke	China
Age of degenerative and man-made diseases	35-55	All forms of stroke, ischemic heart disease at relatively young ages	Urban India, Formerly Socialist Economies
Age of delayed degenerative diseases	<50	Stroke and ischemic heart disease, at older ages	Western Europe, North America, Australia/ N.Z.

TABLE 1-2. NUMBER OF DEATHS (IN THOUSANDS) DUE TO SPECIFIC CARDIOVASCULAR DISEASES BY REGIONS OF THE WORLD. 1990*

Region	Number of Deaths in Thousands				
	Rheumatic	Inflammatory	Other	Cerebrovascular	Ischemic
Established Market Economies	20	65	633	788	1 688
Formerly Socialist Economies	25	39	341	639	1 027
India	70	83	490	448	1 175
China	163	66	305	1 272	762
Other Asia and Islands	10	82	406	390	461
Sub Saharan Africa	20	63	140	383	209
Latin America and Caribbean	8	25	160	249	348
Middle Eastern Crescent	24	72	377	212	610

*Reference 15

that these areas are diminishing in size and are increasingly limited to rural areas. A clear challenge is to complete the "unfinished agenda," namely the control of infectious, parasitic, nutritional, and perinatal diseases, while looking forward to additional problems predictable with transition to the next phase.

As these communicable diseases are controlled, a next phase is the increase in CVD mortality to 10–35% of deaths, and with hypertension-related diseases (e.g. hypertensive heart disease, stroke) contributing to the additional mortality. In several regions of the world, such as China and Korea, stroke is the leading cause of death (Table 1-2). In others, including Africa, cerebrovascular disease exceeds ischemic heart disease. Populations genetically predisposed to hypertension or environmentally exposed to dietary factors such as heavy salt intake would be affected in particular. In Western countries, urbanization and industrialization has been associated with a fall in stroke rates, predating therapies to treat hypertension.

The next phase in which the CVD epidemic becomes fully expressed is the "age of degenerative and man-made diseases." In this instance, ischemic heart disease and stroke occur at relatively young ages, certainly earlier than 50 years of age. This peak in the epidemic now accounts for one third to over half of deaths. This phase appears to be well established in Russia and the former Socialist economies in eastern Europe (Table 1-2). These countries have the highest CVD rates in the world at present, and may even be considered to be regressing from a pattern of delayed degenerative disease to one with increasing heart disease and stroke mortality, and falling life expectancy (4–6). Of the extraordinary fall in life expectancy in Russian men from 63.8 years in 1990 to 57.7 years in 1994, 33% was due to increases in CVD (6). Another region of concern is South Asia, especially India, which appears to be emerging into this phase. While vital statistics are not available, the increasing prevalence of CVD patients occupying Indian hospitals supports the contention that CVD is a growing problem (7).

The final phase of the epidemiologic transition finds cardiovascular disease still accounting for almost half of mortality, but at advanced ages. Western Europe, North America, Australia and New Zealand have all witnessed sizable declines in their age-adjusted CVD mortality rates (8). While CVD will likely remain a major cause of death, the ability to reduce its impact in persons of economically productive ages has been well documented.

While a country may experience an overall trend, either upwards or downwards, it is useful to note that subpopulations may vary in their adoption of a new disease pattern. In this context, the concept of early versus late adopter communities may be useful to describe patterns within a country (Figure 1-1) (9). An early adopter community may take up deleterious health behaviors early on, only to suffer the consequences earlier. It should not be assumed that this cross-section represents a stable pattern, however. As these early adopter communities absorb health

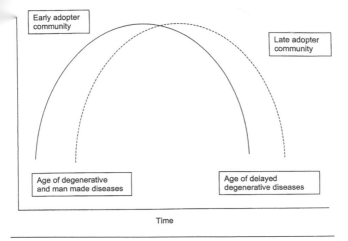

Fig 1-1. *Schematic diagram of CVD Mortality in Emerging vs Late Adopter Communities at Various Times in the Epidemiologic Transition.*

promotion messages, their CVD mortality rates may peak and even decline. However, slow adopter communities which receive and react to trends more slowly may develop comparable CVD rates at a time later than the early adopters. Since they are slower to correct them, their rates are relatively higher at a later time point. This may explain observations in the 1970s that African American and rural populations appeared protected from CVD in the US, only to find their rates higher than whites and urban dwellers in the 1990s (10). One implication is that, even within a developing country, there are likely to be affluent, well-educated subpopulations at later phases in the epidemiologic transition. These populations will need services different from the community as a whole.

MYTHS ABOUT THE CURRENT BURDEN OF CARDIOVASCULAR DISEASE WORLDWIDE, WITH AN EMPHASIS ON DEVELOPING COUNTRIES

Concerns about the growing problem of CVD in developing countries began to emerge in the late 1980s or early 1990s, when growing proportions of hospital beds in developing countries began to be occupied by cases of CVD (11) and a variety of projections and trends made it eminently clear that a CVD epidemic was almost inevitable (12-14). The recently published Global Burden of Disease Study appears to confirm these projections (15). This analysis estimates that CVD had become the leading cause of death in the World by 1990 (Table 1-3). More interestingly, the data suggest that CVD and infectious and parasitic diseases have similar burdens of mortality for developing countries in 1990. Note that far more CVD deaths occur in developing than developed countries. With the rising rates of CV mortality, and the falling rates due to parasites and in

TABLE 1-3. Deaths in Developed and Developing
Countries from Top Ten Causes in 1990

| | Deaths in Thousands in Region | | |
Cause of Death	Developed	Developing	World
Cardiovascular disorders	5 245	9 082	14 327
Infectious and parasitic diseases	163	9 166	9 329
Malignant neoplasms	2 413	3 611	6 024
Respiratory infections	389	3 992	4 380
Unintentional injuries	552	2 682	3 233
Respiratory disorders	500	2 435	2 935
Perinatal disorders	82	2 361	2 443
Digestive disorders	424	1 426	1 851
Intentional injuries	282	1 569	1 851
Genitourinary disorders	167	568	735

Reference 15.

tions, it can be safely surmised that the current state of
affairs finds CVD to be the leading cause of mortality even
in developing countries. In fact, noncommunicable disease
deaths exceed infectious and parasitic diseases in all regions
of the world except Sub Saharan Africa and the Middle
East.

Despite these projections, a number of international
health agencies and foundations have attempted to disre-
gard CVD as a health problem, in favor of more traditional
concerns for infectious, parasitic, nutritional and childhood
diseases. For example, the World Health Organization, in
the preliminary publication entitled: "Health for All in the
21st Century," makes virtually no mention of CVD as a
growing threat, with a continued emphasis on childhood
and infectious diseases (16). A number of myths have been
put forward to rationalize the overlooking of CVD, including the notions that CVD is a disease limited to the elderly,
to men, and to the rich, that CVD is not a cause of disability due to its rapid mortality and that curtailing the CVD
epidemic is impossible. More recent data can be used to
refute these myths (15). For example, while age and male
sex are risk factors for CVD, it does not mean that CVD
spares younger persons and women (Table 1-4). An analysis of deaths in economically productive years, ages 30 to
69 years, shows CVD deaths to exceed those from infectious
and parasitic diseases in all populations except Sub-Saharan
Africa and even there, the two are almost equal. While the
numbers of deaths due to CVD are generally lower for
women than for men, the same mortality excess of CVD
over infectious and parasitic causes remains true in women,
again during the economically and socially productive
years.

Is CVD only a disease of the rich? While upper income
and educational strata, as early adopters, may be affected
by CVD early in the transition, it is presumptuous to
believe that CVD does not eventually affect the poorly edu-
cated and low income strata. In fact, in countries in the last
phase of the epidemic, this lower socioeconomic strata has
strikingly higher CVD mortality rates (17,18). This pattern
s been replicated in most North American and European

TABLE 1-4. DEATHS DUE TO CARDIOVASCULAR DISEASE (CVD) AND TO INFECTIONS AND PARASITIC DISEASES (IPD) IN 30–69 YEAR OLDS BY SEX AND REGION IN 1990*

Region	Deaths in Thousands			
	Men		Women	
	CVD	IPD	CVD	IPD
Established Market European	483	42	227	12
Formerly Socialist Economies	263	20	163	6
India	611	429	481	240
China	576	158	439	89
Other Asia and Island	289	147	226	140
Sub Saharan Africa	183	215	211	228
Latin American and Caribbean	186	62	147	48
Middle Eastern Crescent	285	83	215	85
World	3 028	1 128	2 201	798

* Derived from reference 15.

countries as part of their transition into the fourth phase (19).

One important feature of the work by Murray and Lopez has been their use of Disability Adjusted Life Years (DALYs) as a measure not only of mortality, but also of disability. Using this measure, CVD ranks fourth in 1990 after infectious and parasitic diseases, neuropsychiatric disorders, and injuries (20) (Table 1-5). However, projections to 2020 show different results (see below), with CVD becoming a major cause of disability and death in all parts of the world (18,21).

Can the CVD epidemic be curtailed in developing countries? Certainly, the plummeting rates of heart disease and stroke in developed countries suggest that the epidemic is treatable (8,21). Moreover, there are anecdotal reports of some developing countries, such as Costa Rica, in which rising CVD rates flattened and declined after investment in health and education. There seems little support to the idea that attempts to blunt the rise in CVD will be unrewarded.

TABLE 1-5. PERCENT OF DISABILITY ADJUSTED LIFE YEARS ATTRIBUTABLE TO SPECIFIC CAUSES OF DEATH FOR DEVELOPED AND DEVELOPING PARTS OF THE WORLD, 1990*

	% of Total DALYS in 1990		
Disorder Group	Developed	Developing	World
Infectious and parasitic diseases	2.7	25.6	22.9
Neuropsychiatric disorders	22.0	9.0	10.5
Unintentional injuries	10.3	11.1	11.0
Cardiovascular diseases	20.4	8.3	9.7
Respiratory infections	1.6	9.4	8.5
Perinatal disorders	1.9	7.3	6.7
Malignant neoplasms	13.7	4.0	5.1
Respiratory disorders	4.8	4.3	4.4
Intentional injuries	4.2	4.1	4.1
Nutritional deficiencies	0.9	4.1	3.7

* Reference 20

Projections of Cardiovascular Disea. Mortality to the Year 2020

With demographic assumptions as to the size, age distribution and life expectancy of the regional populations, Murray and Lopez have projected the burden of CVD to the year 2020 (22). These projections are a useful means to attempt to plan for and organize disease control efforts. This is especially true for chronic diseases whose basic disease processes begin decades before the onset of symptomatic disease. These models document ischemic heart disease and cerebrovascular disease to be the first and second ranked causes of death currently in 1990 as well as projected for 2020. Diarrheal disease, perinatal conditions, and measles, will all drop out of the top 10 as causes of death worldwide. When developed and developing countries are separated and ranked according to Disability Adjusted Life Years attributable to specific causes (Table 1-6), ischemic heart disease ranks third and cerebrovascular disease ranks fifth in developing countries. When further broken down by region, the relative contributions of infectious/parasitic diseases versus cardiovascular disease can be compared (Figure 1-2). CVD exceeds infectious and parasitic diseases as a cause of death and disability in all regions except Sub Saharan Africa, with 15% or more of DALYS attributable to CVD worldwide. Certainly, the data warrant attention to CVD as a major area of concern based on these demographic assumptions.

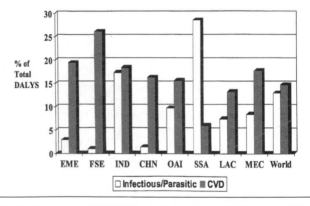

Fig 1-2. *Percentage of DALYS for Infectious/Parasitic Diseases and for Cardiovascular Projected to Year 2020 by Region*.*

Potential Mechanisms which may Cause the Burden of Cardiovascular Disease to be Underestimated

The projections of Murray and Lopez are largely based on increases in life expectancy and population size, but also include income and education, as well as level of smoking (22). While these provide a firm basis for projection, the possibility that these projections may be over- or under estimated should be considered. While development of the economic, educational, and healthcare infrastructure of developing countries may improve dramatically, a variety

TABLE 1-6. TEN PROJECTED LEADING CAUSES OF DALYS IN 2020* AND MILLIONS OF DALYS CAUSED

Rank	Developed Countries		Developing Countries	
	Cause	DALYS	Cause	DALYS
1	Ischemic Heart Disease	18.0	Unipolar Depression	68.8
2	Cerebrovascular Disease	9.9	Traffic Accidents	64.4
3	Unipolar Depression	9.8	Ischemic Heart Disease	64.3
4	Trach/Broch/Lung CA	7.3	COPD	52.7
5	Traffic Accidents	6.9	Cerebrovascular Disease	51.5
6	Alcohol Use	6.1	Tuberculosis	42.4
7	Osteoarthritis	5.6	Lower Resp. Infections	41.1
8	Dementia	5.5	War Injuries	40.2
9	COPD	4.9	Diarrheal Diseases	37.0
10	Self-Inflicted Injury	3.9	HIV	34.0

* Reference 22

TABLE 1-7. REASONS TO EXPECT AN INCREASE IN
    CARDIOVASCULAR DISEASE
    MORTALITY IN DEVELOPING COUNTRIES, 1998 − 2020.

* Population expansion
* Increase in life expectancy
* Deprivation in utero and in childhood
* Use of disposable income for deleterious health behaviors
* Interaction between risk factors
* Interactions between genes and behaviors

of other factors may be considered to suggest that the projections to year 2020 may be underestimates (Table 1-7).

Paradoxically, the more rapid and thorough the control of infectious and parasitic diseases, the more dominant the noncommunicable disease pattern will become. The increasing survival of the population leads both to population expansion and to increased life expectancy, leading to increases in persons in the age strata prone to CVD, namely 40+ years. While developed countries will have large increases in elderly populations (age 70 years and older), developing countries will witness large increases in persons 40 to 70 years (22). While these demographic shifts are included in the models of the Global Burden of Disease Study, reduced mortality from infectious diseases such as malaria and AIDS may have a large effect on those eligible to develop CVD.

A theory applied largely to European and North American populations may have profound implications for the developing world. Barker et al has made the observation that persons with low birth weight or a reduced growth in early childhood are at risk for developing CVD many years later (23,24). In a cohort of 6 500 men born from 1911–1930, those who weighed 18 pounds or less at one year of age had almost three times the cumulative risk of ischemic heart disease than did those men who weighed 27 pounds or more at one year. A variety of mechanisms have been proposed, including the development of factors predisposing those stunted in utero or in early childhood to development of obesity, hypertension, and glucose intolerance (24). If this theory pertains to developing countries as well, sizable numbers of persons stunted by early developmental deficiencies due to nutrition and infection may now be living to the ages in which CVD can manifest itself. The World Health Organization established in 1990 that 1.3 billion persons worldwide are stunted, with almost 40% of Africans and 48% of Southeast Asians identified as stunted (25). If in fact they carry a three-fold increased risk of CVD, prior models may seriously underestimate the burden of disease. Furthermore, one or two generations of adequate in utero and childhood nutrition may be needed before this risk abates.

A potentially more preventable cause of an underestimate of CVD is the extent to which disposable income is used to acquire deleterious health behaviors, including tobacco, a diet rich in fat, cholesterol, sodium, and calories, sedentary lifestyle, and heavy alcohol consumption. Some of the models take into consideration tobacco use, but the

of tobacco in the epidemic of noncommunicable dis-
es cannot be emphasized enough. By 2020, 12% of death
d 9% of DALYS will be attributable to tobacco alone,
with the most striking tobacco-related increases occurring
in developing countries (26,27). Popkin (28) has coined the
term, nutritional transition, to track the changes in a society's eating patterns in parallel with the epidemiologic transition. China provides an opportunity to examine these
effects of CVD risk, as that country has both urban and
rural populations with varying incomes. In studies over
only a three year period, 1989 to 1991, Chinese populations
who lived in urban settings and who had increased income
consumed more fat, reduced their physical activity, and
showed striking increases in the prevalence of being overweight. The physiological correlates of a high fat diet,
sedentarism, and obesity, namely hyperlipidemia, hypertension, and diabetes, should be expected to follow.

Many of the projections of CVD mortality did not take
into account the interaction between CVD risk factors. It is
well known that multiple risk factors coexisting in the same
person interact to multiply the risk (29). Therefore, the
impact of an increase in one risk factor may be magnified
by the presence of others. Consider the scenario of North-
ern China, which has a high incidence of hypertension and
extraordinary 75% prevalence of smoking in men (30), but
relatively low serum cholesterol levels. If the diet changes
considerably with increases in the amount of fat and cholesterol, the serum cholesterol level can be expected to rise. As
compared to a population with low rates of hypertension
and smoking, the rates of CVD in hypertensive smokers
might be expected to increase remarkably in both relative
and absolute terms. These risk factor interactions may make
the generalization of the magnitude of CVD increases difficult, and may require a country-by-country analysis.

Finally, changes in health behaviors in a country may
have varying effects on CVD rates due to genetic heterogeneity of the population. This gene-environment interaction
suggests that a health behavior may have a minor impact
in one genetically defined population only to have a major
effect on CVD rates in another. A prototype for this concept
is the "thrifty genotype," hypothesized by Neal to confer a
survival advantage during times of famine by making efficient the storage of fat through an oversecretion of insulin
postprandially (31). This gene then becomes detrimental in
times of positive caloric balance by predisposing the person
to obesity, hyperinsulinism, and diabetes. A variety of
populations are felt to be susceptible to CVD on this basis,
including Asian Indians (32). In fact, persons from India,
Pakistan, and other Southern Asian countries appear to
have an excess of diabetes, low HDL cholesterol, and higher
triglycerides (33,34). Even modest changes in body weight
appear related to increased CVD risk. In fact, South Asians
who emigrate to Europe, North America, South Africa, etc.,
have markedly increased risks of CVD, exceeding those of
their adopted countries (35). In the US, Asian Indians arg
ably have the highest CVD rates of any ethnic minorit
the behavioral factors which induced this, namely hig

orie diet and sedentarism become prevalent in the In₍
subcontinent, it might be predictable that an exaggera₍
CVD epidemic may occur. There appears to be some ev₍
dence for the emergence of such a major health problem
even now, and the CVD projections for this populous
region may be underestimated. A broader conclusion may
be that the CVD epidemic may look very different from
one country to the next, for a variety of reasons, one of
them being genetic. The need to tailor interventions to the
local epidemiology of CVD may need to be based on such
factors.

RESEARCH AND DEVELOPMENT
OPPORTUNITIES FOR CARDIOVASCULAR
DISEASE CONTROL

Ischemic heart disease and stroke mortality rates have
declined up to 50% in developed countries, suggesting that
the available preventive and case-management strategies
can be effective. The challenge then is to determine if they
are applicable to the CVD of developing countries, whether
they can be implemented in these diverse settings, and
whether CVD rates are in fact reduced by these actions. Primordial prevention, the prevention of the development of
risk factors, may be especially promising to countries at the
early stages of the epidemiologic transition. This is especially true if limited health sector resources are available for
treatment of established risk factors and CVD.

A major barrier to implementation is the dearth of
basic data on the epidemiology of CVD, i.e., prevalence,
incidence, risk factors, and natural history of ischemic heart
disease and stroke in developing countries in general, and
on a regional or country-by-country basis in particular. In
many instances, the Global Burden of Disease Study relied
on projections and less on data to estimate mortality and
DALYS associated with CVD. A key epidemiologic statistic
which is badly needed for program planning is the population attributable risk fraction for each risk factor. This estimates the proportion of CVD due to each risk factor in the
population, using its prevalence and the relative risk for
disease associated with the risk factor. This will require
local cross-sectional surveys, case-control studies, and even
prospective studies to better define the prevalences of both
CVD and its risk factors and the relation of that country's
risk factors to CVD. Ways to standardize and control qual-
ity of risk factor measurements must be given priority.
New field methods, such as rapid epidemiologic surveys
and verbal autopsies, may need to be applied to areas in
which vital statistics are unreliable.

While the risk factor paradigm has been rather robust
in its generalizability to various population groups, the possibility of new risk factors, as yet to be defined, should be
ɔnsidered. New infectious etiologies of CVD (e.g., chlamy-
ˑl infections) and effects of nutrition and human develop-
t on CVD may be uniquely investigated in developing
ˑries.

As each society identifies priorities for CVD control, ...dies of interventions which modify human behavior at .he individual, community, and national level need to be carried out. Community interventions may have a unique role to play in developing countries, as a way to target high risk subgroups to convert them from slow to rapid adopters of risk behavior change. It seems that many of the interventions will need to be developed and tested locally, after adapting them to be appropriate to local cultures and resources. There may be some overarching interventions that are more generalizable, including the use of taxation and other means of raising price and reducing access to deleterious health behaviors. Similarly, if occasional clinical trials of risk factor modification or case management of established CVD were carried out in developing countries, their generalizability to other developing countries might be easier, not only on the basis of efficacy but also on cost-effectiveness and efficiency.

In lieu of country-specific research findings, can recommendations be made at this point for prevention of CVD in developing countries? Certainly, the need for tobacco control requires no further study, and countries should regulate tobacco accessibility, limit its use through taxation, and educate the population as to its profound contribution to death and disability. A major concern currently is the possibility of settlements of health claims with the US government. While penalizing the multinational tobacco companies for health effects in the US, the concern is that the US will become a safe haven for these companies, who will thereafter be immune from further prosecution. It appears that every country may need to implement these legal actions. Similarly, national policies on nutrition and transportation should be examined as means for primordial prevention. Finally, risk factor control programs, including detection of hypertension and hyperlipidemia, may be worthwhile in those countries in which the attributable risk fractions for these risk factors is high.

A major opportunity exists in selecting cost effective approaches to the case management of ischemic heart disease and stroke. Current guidelines for secondary prevention need not be expensive (36). Risk factor modification including smoking cessation, a low fat/cholesterol diet, exercise, and weight control do not require costly technologies. Aspirin and beta blockers are also both inexpensive and ubiquitous. The impressive literature supporting the use of lipid-lowering agents in secondary prevention may require the identification of an inexpensive agent for use in high risk patients, on a cost effective basis. In general, the major benefits of developed countries' secondary prevention guidelines can be reaped without expensive technology or technical staff. At the same time, the use of high technology in CVD case management is the hallmark of developed country cardiology. For most subgroups of patients, coror ary artery bypass, angioplasty, stenting, and other expe sive and invasive procedures have not been shown tc efficacious or cost effective, when compared with cur available medical management. "State-of-the-art needs redefinition, to emphasize preventive interventic (37) and to avoid huge capital and personal investments o. cost-ineffective interventions.

A variety of activities have been initiated by international agencies to begin to deal with this problem. The International Societies and Federations of Cardiology have developed a White Paper on CVD as a Global Health Problem and have created a Task Force on Risk Factors in Developing Countries. An allied group, the Global Cardiovascular Disease Interest Group, has developed a focused interest on the role of cardiovascular specialty societies in curtailing the CVD epidemic (38). The notion is that specialists in cardiovascular medicine must support if not lead country-wide CVD control efforts. Several groups have developed guidelines for risk factor management in CVD cases and in other high risk persons. These groups include the European Consortium (European Society of Cardiology, European Atherosclerosis Society, and European Society of Hypertension), an International Task Force for Prevention of Coronary Heart Disease, and the American Heart Association. Perhaps the most promising is an effort by the Institute of Medicine in the United States to develop a report on the Research, Development, and Institutional Strengthening for Control of Cardiovascular Diseases in Developing Countries. This report, due to be released in mid 1998, will be used as a background document by a forum convened by the World Bank for agencies which fund international health projects. Hopefully, a global effort on CVD control will spring from these efforts.

CONCLUSIONS

Africa may have a curious advantage in being at an earlier state of the epidemiologic transition. Infectious, parasitic, nutritional, and perinatal diseases appear to be chronic problems; the AIDS epidemic is especially worrisome. These major challenges of the unfinished agenda clearly need attention. However, it may also be worthwhile to look beyond to the next challenges (39). There looms the impending CVD epidemic. Developing countries should take the advantage conferred by history. The experience gained from the control of an epidemic of CVD in North America, Western Europe and Australia/New Zealand should be applied to developing countries. Unfortunately, such a preventive intervention was not possible in Eastern Europe and Russia. In order for these lessons to be applied, there must be a recognition on the part of policy makers, educators, clinicians, and researchers that the threat exists. Procrastination until the CVD epidemic is fully established is likely not the best approach.

SUMMARY

burden of cardiovascular disease (CVD), especially ic heart disease and stroke, varies remarkably ween regions of the world, with declining rates in Europe, North America, and Australia/New Zealand, burgeoning epidemics in the former Socialist economies and India, and relatively lower impact in developing regions such as Sub Saharan Africa.

The basis for a prediction of a global CVD epidemic lies in the "epidemiologic transition," in which control of infectious, parasitic, and nutritional diseases allows most of the population to reach the ages in which CVD manifests itself. In fact, CVD is already the leading cause of death not only in developed countries but, as of the mid 1990s, developing countries as well. A variety of myths have attempted to minimize the rationale for CVD control in developing countries. In reality, CVD does not only affect men, the elderly, or the rich, but a broad spectrum of the population. Moreover, as a cause of disability it will be a world leader by 2020. Finally, there is evidence that the epidemic can be curtailed.

Projections to the year 2020 predict an expansion of the CVD epidemic to the developing world, with CVD exceeding infectious and parasitic diaereses in all regions except Sub Saharan Africa. These estimates in fact may be conservative, since several factors may allow multiplication of risk. In utero or early childhood deprivation, the use of disposable income for deleterious health behaviors (such as tobacco and a high fat/cholesterol diet), interactions between multiple co-existing risk factors, and the interaction between newly acquired health behaviors and genes may all inflate the risk to levels above those predicted.

Efforts to control CVD should invest strategically in research to understand the prevalence of and risks associated with CVD risk factors, as well as in studies of new risk factors, modifications to prevent or modify risk, and clinical trials to demonstrate efficacy of these interventions. In lieu of this improved research base, a number of initiatives should go forward to prevent the dissemination of risk factors, to treat risk factors appropriately in high risk subjects, and to develop case management strategies shown to be both efficacious and cost-effective. A global epidemic of CVD in developing countries may be inevitable, unless there is a better understanding of its origins, a prediction of its magnitude, and the organization of preventive and case management strategies early enough to control it.

References

1. Omram AR. The epidemiologic transition: A theory of the epidemiology of population change. *Milbank Memorial Fund Quarterly* 1971; 49:509-38.

2. Preston SH. *Mortality Patterns in Human Populations, with Special Reference to Recorded Causes of Death*. New York: Academic Press, 1976.

3. Olshansky SJ, Ault AB. The fourth stage of the epidemiol transition: The age of delayed degenerative diseases. *Milbank orial Fund Quarterly* 1986; 64:355–91.

4. Marmot M, Kogevinus M, Elston MA: Socioeconomic s

disease. In Health Promotion Research: *Towards a New Social Epi* *miology*. Copenhagen: WHO Regional Publications, European Serie No 37, 1991.

5. Bobadilla JL, Costello CA, Mitchell F (Eds). *Premature Death in the Newly Independent States*. Washington, DC: National Academy Press, 1997.

6. Notzon FC, Komarov YM, et al. Causes of declining life expectancy in Russia. *JAMA* 1998; 279:793–800.

7. Reddy KS. Cardiovascular disease in India. *World Health Stat Q*. 1993:46:101–107.

8. Thom TJ. International mortality from heart disease: Rates and trends. *Int. J. Epidemiol*. 1989; 18:S20–S28.

9. Stone EJ, Pearson TA, et al. Community-based prevention trials: Challenges and directions for public health practice, policy, and research. *Ann Epidemiol* 1997; S7:S113–S120.

10. Winkleby MA. Acclerating cardiovascular risk factor change in ethnic minority and low socioeconomic groups. *Am Epidemiol* 1997,S7:S96–S103.

11. Dodu SRA. Emergence of cardiovascular diseases in developing countries. *Cardiology* 1988; 75:56–64.

12. Pearson TA, Jamison DT, Trejo-Gutierrez J. Cardiovascular diseases. In Jamison DT, Mosley WH, et al (Eds). *Disease Control Priorities in Developing Countries*. New York, NY: Oxford University Press; 1993.

13. Whelton PK, Brancati FC, Appel LJ, Klag MJ. The challenge of hypertension and atherosclerotic cardiovascular disease in economically developing countries. *High Blood Pressure* 1995; 4:36–45.

14. Reddy KS, Yusuf S. Emerging epidemic of cardiovascular disease in developing countries. *Circulation* 1998; 97:596-601.

15. Murray CJL, Lopez AD, eds. *The global burden of disease:* A comprehensive assessment of mortality and disability from diseases, injuries, and risk factors in 1990 and projected to 2020. Cambridge: Harvard University Press, 1996.

16. World Health Organization. *Health for All in the 21st Century*. Geneva: WHO, 1998.

17. Kaplan GA, Keil JE, Socioeconomic factors and cardiovascular disease: a review of the literature. *Circulation* 1993; 88:1973-1998.

18. Rose G, Marmot MG. Social class and coronary heart disease. *Br. Heart J*. 1981; 45:13–19.

19. Kunst AE, Groenhof F, Mackenback J. et al. Differences between occupational classes in cardiovascular disease mortality: A comparison of 11 European Countries, In: *Report of the Conference in Socioeconomic status and Cardiovascular Health and Disease*. Bethesda: National Heart, Lung, and Blood Institute, 1996, pp 49-56.

20. Murray CJL, Lopez AD. Global mortality, disability, and the contribution of risk factors: Global Burden of Disease Study. *Lancet* 1997; 349:1436–42.

21. Higgins M, Thom T. Trends in CHD in the United States. *Int J of Epidemiol*, 1989; 18:S58–S66.

Murray CJL, Lopez AD. Alternative projections of mortality disability by cause 1990–2020: Global Burden of Disease Study. *t* 1997; 349:1498–1504.

ker DJP, Winter PD, Osmond C, et al. Weight in infancy and om ischemic heart disease. In: DJP Barker (ed): Fetal and int Origins of Adult Disease. London: *British Medical Journal* '92; 141–49.

24. Barker DJP, Osmond C. Infant mortality, childhood nutrition, and ischemic heart disease in England and Wales. In DJP Barker (ed): Fetal and Infant Origins of Adult Disease. London: *British Medical Journal*, 1992:23–27.

25. Mosley WH, Gray R. Childhood precursors of adult morbidity and mortality in developing countries: Implications for health programs. In Gribble JN, Preston SH (Eds): *The Epidemiological Transition*. Washington DC. The National Academy Press, pp 69–100.

26. Peto R, Lopez AD, et al. *Mortality from smoking in developed countries 1950-2000*: Indirect estimates from National Vital Statistics. Oxford: Oxford University Press, 1994.

27. Peto R, Lopez AD, et al. Mortality from smoking worldwide. *Br Med Bull* 1996; 52:12–25.

28. Popkin BM. The nutrition transition in low-income countries: An emerging crisis. *Nutrition Reviews* 1994; 52:285–298.

29. Blackburn H. The concept of risk. In: Pearson TA, Criqui M, et al (Eds). *Primer in Preventive Cardiology*. Dallas: American Heart Association. 1994; pp 25–41.

30. Yuan J-M, Ross RK, et al. Morbidity and mortality in relation to cigarette smoking in Shanghai, China. *JAMA* 1996; 275:1646–1650.

31. Neel JV. The Thrifty Gene. *Am J Human Genet* 1962; 14:353–362.

32. Zimmet PZ. Challenges in diabetes epidemiology—From West to the Rest. *Diabetes Care* 1992; 15:232–252.

33. McKeigue PM, Ferie JE, Pierpoint T, Marmot, MG. Association of early-onset coronary heart disease in South Asian men with glucose intolerance and hyperinsulinism. *Circulation* 1993; 87:152–161.

34. Enas EA, Garg A, et al. Coronary heart disease and its risk factors in first-generation immigrant Asian Indians to the United States of America. *Indian Heart J* 1996; 48:343–353.

35. Enas EA, Yusuf S, Mehta D. Prevalence of coronary artery disease in Asian Indians. *Am J. Cardiol.* 1992; 70:945–949.

36. Smith SC, Blair SN, Criqui MH et al. Preventing heart attack and death in patients with coronary disease. *Circulation* 1995; 92:2–4.

37. Fuster V, Pearson TA (Eds): 27th Bethesda Conference: Matching the intensity of risk factor management with the hazard for coronary disease events. *JACC* 1996; 27:957–1047.

38. Pearson TA, Smith SC Jr, Poole-Wilson P. Cardiovascular specialty societies and the emerging global burden of cardiovascular disease. A call to action. *Circulation* 1998; 97:602–604.

39. Muna WFT. Cardiovascular disorders in Africa. *World Health Statist Quart* 1993; 46:125–133.

CHAPTER 2

West of Scotland and beyond: Looking at Lipids across the Atlantic

Stuart M. Cobbe

THE CHOLESTEROL CONTROVERSY

"A week is a long time in politics"—
Harold Wilson, former British Prime Minister

Writing in 1998, it now seems almost inconceivable that the "cholesterol controversy" was raging in the columns of major journals as recently as the early 1990s (Davey Smith and Pekkanen, 1992; Oliver, 1991; Hulley et al. 1992). In brief, the basis for the controversy rested on the inadequate evidence for the benefit and safety of cholesterol reduction in the prevention of coronary heart disease (CHD) events. The association between elevated levels of total, and particularly low-density lipoprotein (LDL) cholesterol and increased risk of atherosclerotic coronary heart disease and coronary death has been established to the satisfaction of most investigators over many years (La Rosa et al. 1990). Early clinical trials of cholesterol reduction by diet or drugs had shown, in meta-analysis, a significant reduction in the risk of fatal and non-fatal myocardial infarction (Davey Smith and Pekkanen, 1992; Law et al. 1996). However, since individual trials had not been able to demonstrate significant reductions in coronary mortality, the sceptics remained unconvinced. Some of the principal reasons for the failure to achieve reductions in coronary mortality in early trials are listed in Table 2-1.

There have been major advances in the science of clinical trial design during the last 30 years, and most of the early trials were underpowered by modern standards. Hence there was a considerable risk of Type II error, resulting in false-negative conclusions. In addition, the statistical methods applied in some cases would not meet current standards. For example, The Lipid Research Clinics Coronary Primary Prevention Trial (1984) reported a significant 19% relative risk reduction in the incidence of its pr

TABLE 2-1. LIMITATIONS IN EARLY TRIALS OF CORONARY PREVENTION

Insufficient sample size
Low-risk populations in study
Small reduction in total/LDL cholesterol
Inadequate duration of follow-up
Toxic/poorly tolerated lipid-lowering intervention

endpoint of non-fatal myocardial infarction or coronary heart disease death using a single-sided p value ($p<0.05$). The 90% confidence intervals for the risk reduction were 3%–32%. Currently, major journals such as the New England Journal of Medicine require the principal results of clinical trials to be expressed using two-sided statistical tests, with 95% rather than 90% confidence intervals. On this basis, the principal result of the LRC-CPPT would have been non-significant.

Size of cholesterol reduction

The epidemiological evidence indicates a continuous association between total or LDL cholesterol levels and risk both within and between populations (Keys, 1980; Stamler et al. 1986; Chen et al. 1991). For this risk to be reduced, a significant decrease in cholesterol levels must be achieved and maintained for an adequate period. An insufficiently powerful cholesterol-lowering intervention is unlikely, therefore, to produce a significant beneficial result. This may be as a result of intrinsic lack of efficacy, or to poor tolerability due to adverse effects or inconvenience of administration. Peto and colleagues (1985) subdivided the early trials according to the magnitude of cholesterol reduction, and confirmed the "dose-response" relationship between lipid reduction and coronary prevention. Poor compliance is likely to have been a major factor in many of the dietary trials, especially those undertaken on unselected free-living populations. For example, the World Health Organisation European Collaborative Group (1986) showed significant reductions in coronary end-points in some countries (e.g. Belgium) where compliance was good and risk factors were reduced. In contrast, the British limb of this trial showed no reductions either in risk factor levels or in coronary incidence.

Duration of trial

Epidemiological studies of the relationship between cholesterol and CHD risk are, in effect, comparing the effect of many decades' exposure to high versus low cholesterol levels. It should not necessarily be assumed that the effects of prolonged hypercholesterolaemia can be rapidly reversed. Thus cholesterol-lowering trials of brief duration ay underestimate the effects of therapy, and reductions in onary events may not appear until a "lag period" has ed. This concept was supported in meta-analyses by t al (1985) and Law et al (1996). It was found that rials of at least 5 years duration were necessary before the epidemiologically predicted reduction in coronary events began to be seen. A number of the larger early studies also showed a delay of 2–3 years before evidence of benefit from cholesterol reduction appeared (The Lipid Research Clinics Coronary Primary Prevention Trial, 1984; Frick et al. 1987; Buchwald et al. 1990).

Non-cardiovascular mortality

Although the weight of evidence available by the early 1990s indicated that cholesterol reduction could reduce CHD risk, considerable concern existed as to the possible adverse effect of cholesterol reduction on non-cardiovascular mortality. This was associated in the minds of many with the inverse epidemiological association between cholesterol levels and non-cardiovascular death, which results in there being a virtually flat relationship between total cholesterol and all-cause mortality (Isles et al. 1989; Jacobs et al. 1992). In reality, the levels of cholesterol achieved by treatment of hypercholesterolaemic subjects with the therapies available at that time were still well above those associated with increased non-cardiovascular risk in epidemiologial studies. Nevertheless, a concern persisted in the minds of many, and was reinforced by the results of the largest of the early (non-statin) primary prevention trials (Committee of Principal Investigators, 1984; The Lipid Research Clinics Coronary Primary Prevention Trial, 1984; Frick et al. 1987). These results were assembled into a meta-analysis which suggested that the significant aggregate effect of cholesterol reduction in primary prevention of coronary disease was offset by trends toward increases in cancer deaths and in deaths due to accidents, violence or suicide (Davey Smith and Pekkanen, 1992) (Table 2-2).

TABLE 2-2. META-ANALYSIS OF PRE-STATIN PRIMARY PREVENTION TRIALS

Cause of Death	Diet Studies		Drug Studies	
	Odds Ratio	95% CI	Odds Ratio	95% CI
CHD	0.71	0.55-0.90	0.72	0.55-0.94
Cancer	1.31	0.92-1.86	1.33	0.93-1.89
Injury*	1.20	0.75-1.93	1.75	1.07-2.85
All Causes	0.95	0.82-1.09	1.16	0.98-1.38

*Accidents, suicide or violence
Ref: Davey Smith and Pekkanen, 1992.

THE WEST OF SCOTLAND CORONARY PREVENTION STUDY

The design, baseline characteristics and principal results of the West of Scotland Coronary Prevention Study (WOSCOPS) have been published (West of Scotland Coronary Prevention Study Group, 1992; 1995; Shepherd et a' 1995) and reviewed extensively (Oliver, 1995; Gotto, 199

Oliver et al. 1997). The study was the first to investigate the effects of lipid lowering therapy with an HMG Co-A reductase inhibitor, pravastatin, in primary prevention. The HMG Co-A reductase inhibitors (statins) achieve greater reductions in total and LDL cholesterol levels than achieved with previous drugs, with moderate beneficial effects on triglycerides and high density lipoprotein (HDL) cholesterol levels.

WOSCOPS Principal Results

The subjects randomised into WOSCOPS were men aged 45–64 years of age, with moderate hypercholesterolaemia but no prior evidence of myocardial infarction, coronary revascularisation or other major pathology. The entry criteria were LDL cholesterol levels on diet in the range 4.0–6.0 mmol/l on two occasions, with at least one value $\geqslant 4.5$ mmol/l. The main outcomes of WOSCOPS are presented in Table 2-3. Treatment with pravastatin 40 mg daily for 5 years resulted in a 31% relative reduction in the risk of the primary endpoint of CHD death or non-fatal myocardial infarction ($p<0.001$). The relative risk of cardiovascular death was reduced by 32% ($p=0.033$), and the use of coronary revascularisation procedures by 37% ($p=0.009$). In contrast to the results of the earlier primary prevention studies discussed above, there was no evidence of any adverse effect on non-cardiovascular mortality. The overall effect on all-cause mortality was a relative risk reduction of 22% ($p=0.051$). There was a significant withdrawal rate from the study medication of approximately 15% in the first year, and 3% per annum thereafter. Thus by the end of the study, some 30% of the subjects were no longer receiving trial medication, although none was lost to follow-up. Pravastatin was very well tolerated, with no significant difference in withdrawals from therapy between the active and

TABLE 2-3. WOSCOPS PRINCIPAL RESULTS

Endpoint	Placebo		Pravastatin		P	Risk Reduction (CI)
	(n=3292)		(n=3302)			
	Events	%	Events	%		
Non-fatal MI/CHD Death	248	7.9	174	5.5	<0.001	31 (17 to 43)
CABG/PTCA	80	2.5	51	1.7	0.009	37 (11 to 56)
Cardiovascular Deaths	73	2.3	50	1.6	0.033	32 (3 to 53)
Non-Cardiovascular Deaths	62	1.9	56	1.7	0.54	11 (-28 to 38)
All-Cause Mortality	135	4.1	106	3.2	0.051	22 (0 to 40)

Notes:
Primary endpoint: Definite non-fatal myocardial infarction or coronary heart disease death. CABG/PTCA: First coronary artery bypass grafting or percutaneous transluminal coronary angioplasty. %: Absolute % risk at yr. P values: Based on log-rank test (intention to treat). CI: 95% confidence Intervals. Ref: Shepherd, Cobbe, Ford et al. (1995.)

.acebo groups. No significant excess of liver or muscle .oxicity was seen in the pravastatin treated group. Detailed cause-specific analysis of non-cardiovascular hospital admissions showed no differences between the groups with the exception of a small reduction in hospitalisation for hepato-biliary causes in the pravastatin group (West of Scotland Coronary Prevention Study Group, 1998a).

IMPLICATIONS OF WOSCOPS

"When the evidence changes, I change my opinion"—
Michael Oliver

The publication of WOSCOPS in 1995 confirmed and extended the results of the Scandinavian Simvastatin Survival Study (1994a) in demonstrating the efficacy and safety of statin therapy in both primary and secondary prevention of coronary events. These two trials, with subsequent confirmation by the Cholesterol And Recurrent Events study (Sacks et al. 1996), The Long Term Evaluation of Pravastatin in Ischaemic Disease (Tonkin et al, 1998) and the Air Force/Texas Coronary Prevention study (Downs et al, 1998) have led to general acceptance of the cholesterol hypothesis both in terms of pathogenesis and reversibility of risk. All of the trials have shown statin therapy to be very well tolerated, and none has given any cause for concern in relation to possible increases in non-cardiovascular mortality. Recent meta-analysis, including all of the older trials plus the statin trials, confirms that cholesterol reduction *per se* does not increase non-cardiovascular mortality, but there is an increase in risk specifically associated with fibrates and hormone therapy (Gould et al. 1998).

Risk prediction

Having established the safety and efficacy of statins, the debate has moved on to the issue of selection of patients for treatment. This is by no means a simple matter, given the prevalence of hypercholesterolaemia in Western societies. For example, in the Scottish Heart Health Study (Tunstall-Pedoe et al. 1989), total cholesterol was measured in a randomly selected sample of Scottish adults, and it was found that approximately 40% of men aged 45–64 had a level $\geq$6.5 mmol/l (250 mg/dl). These men would have been potentially eligible for entry into WOSCOPS. Should we now contemplate treating a substantial percentage of all middle-aged and possibly elderly individuals in the community with statins? In order to address this issue, we must bear in mind that coronary atherosclerosis is a disease with a multifactorial aetiology, and that cholesterol (or LDL) levels alone are not an accurate indicator of risk. This is clearly illustrated in Fig 2-1, derived from the screening study of the Multiple Risk Factor Intervention Trial (Stamler et al. 1986). The 356,222 screenees were subdivided into four categories on the basis of smoking and blood pressur

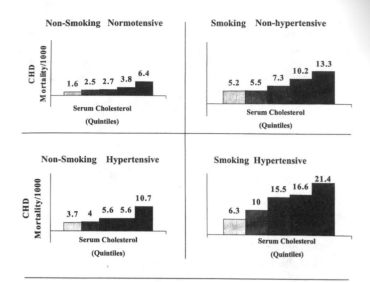

Fig 2-1. *Multiple Risk Factor Intervention screening study (Stamler et al. 1986)*

In each group, the subjects were then subdivided into quintiles of baseline total cholesterol. The 6-year coronary heart disease mortality was determined for each quintile. The clear positive association between cholesterol and CHD risk is seen in each group, with a 2.5–4 fold increase in relative risk from the lowest to the highest quintile. However, it can also be seen that the CHD risk in the lowest quintile of the hypertensive, smoking group is almost identical to the risk in the highest quintile of the normotensive, non-smokers. A policy of treatment with statins based on lipid levels alone may target individuals with isolated hypercholesterolaemia who may be at lower risk than others with moderate cholesterol levels in conjunction with other risk factors. This may result in overtreatment of low-risk subjects and undertreatment of high-risk subjects.

Many multifactorial risk prediction equations have been published, based on epidemiological studies in the United States, Europe, and Britain (Anderson et al. 1991; Assmann & Schulte, 1992; Shaper et al. 1985). We have recently confirmed that the Framingham risk equation adequately predicted the risk in the placebo-treated group of WOSCOPS (West of Scotland Coronary Prevention Study Group, 1998b). A multivariate analysis of the independent baseline predictors of fatal or non-fatal coronary events in WOSCOPS (West of Scotland Coronary Prevention Study Group, 1997) is presented in Table 2-4. Pravastatin therapy was associated with a relative risk of 0.68, i.e. a 32% risk reduction. The proportional hazards assumption was not violated, indicating that the relative reduction in risk achieved by pravastatin therapy was independent of overall risk or of other baseline risk factors. The implications of this are illustrated in Table 2-5, in which the associations between baseline risk, on-therapy risk, absolute risk reduction and the number of patients who need to be treated to prevent one coronary event are shown.

TABLE 2-4. MULTIVARIATE ANALYSIS OF THE INDEPENDENT BASELINE PREDICTORS OF FATAL OR NON-FATAL CORONARY EVENTS IN WOSCOPS

Categorical Variables	% Prevalence	Risk Ratio
Pravastatin Treatment	50	0.68
Current Smoker	44	1.82
Diabetes Mellitus	1.2	2.10
Nitrate Therapy	2.1	1.90
Angina Pectoris	5.1	1.54
FH of Premature CHD	5.7	1.71
Widowed	2.5	1.66
Continuous Variables	**Increment**	**Risk Ratio**
Age	5 years	1.35
Diastolic BP	10 mmHg	1.19
TC/HDL ratio	0.5 units	1.08

Ref: WOSCOPS Study Group 1997

TABLE 2-5. ASSOCIATION BETWEEN BASELINE RISK, ON-THERAPY RISK, ABSOLUTE RISK REDUCTION AND THE NUMBER OF PATIENTS NEEDED TO BE TREATED TO PREVENT ONE CORONARY EVENT

5-year risk of an event %	5	10	15	20
Risk of event on therapy* %	3.4	6.8	10.2	13.6
Absolute risk reduction %	1.6	3.2	4.8	6.4
Number needed to treat	63	31	21	16

* Relative risk reduction 32% independent of baseline risk

The Sheffield Tables

The recognition that cholesterol levels alone are inaccurate predictors of risk, despite the overwhelming evidence linking cholesterol with the pathogenesis of atherosclerosis, is at first sight counter-intuitive. However, such an approach appears to be valid, at least in the prediction of risk in the medium-term (e.g. 5–10 years). A further development of this argument, proposed by Ramsay and colleagues, is that it may not be necessary to measure lipid levels in a substantial proportion of individuals, if they are known to be at low risk by virtue of younger age, absence of clinical atherosclerotic disease or of other risk factors (Ul Haq et al. 1995; Ul Haq et al. 1996; Ramsay et al. 1996). The Sheffield tables, developed by these authors, list the plasma concentration of total cholesterol associated with a pre-specified level of risk, and identify those subjects in whom cholesterol measurement is considered unnecessary. This approach was adopted in the guidelines from the UK Government's Standing Medical Advisory Committee, which proposed that only patients with a 10-year risk of ≥30% (3% per annum) after other risk factor reduction should be treated with statins (Standing Medical Advisory Committee, 1997). The use of the Sheffield tables has been vigorously criticised, on the basis that they make several invalid assumptions, or relegate important clinical subgroups to footnotes (Reynolds, 1997). Thus hypertension is treated a dichotomous variable (present = 160 mmHg, absent = tolic BP 139 mmHg), and a population mean value of

cholesterol is assumed (Ul Haq et al. 1995). The tables d
not take into consideration the possibility of unrecognised
familial hypercholesterolaemia (1 in 200 to 1 in 500), the
effect of family history of CHD, the influence of ethnic origin, particularly in Asians, or the effects of HDL cholesterol
or triglyceride levels.

Health Economics

"Statins work, but can we afford them?"

Much of the debate about the use of statins, particularly in primary prevention, has focused not on safety or
efficacy, but on cost and cost-effectiveness. Given that treatment at present prices may cost several hundred pounds
per annum, the potential impact on National Health Service
budgets is enormous. One study (Pharoah & Hollingworth,
1996) estimated the costs of statin therapy in a Health
authority of 500,000 inhabitants, of whom around 50,000
will be aged 46–64, and around 20,000 will have a total
cholesterol ≥ 6.5 mmol/l. Secondary prevention of post-infarction patients eligible for treatment according to Scandinavian Simvastatin Survival Study criteria was estimated
to cost £4,533,000 over 5 years. To include secondary preventive treatment for men and women with angina, and
primary preventive treatment for WOSCOPS-eligible men
would increase statin costs over 5 years to an estimated
£38,588,000. This particular economic analysis used only the
summary data from SSSS and WOSCOPS, and made a
number of other unverified assumptions. We have recently
published a health economic analysis of WOSCOPS, in
which the costs of cardiovascular events suffered by subjects in the trial were calculated from actual length of stay
and NHS tariffs in the hospitals concerned (Caro et al.
1997). Since the objective of primary prevention is to avoid
or delay the transition from cardiovascular health to disease, we assessed the ability of treatment to prevent the
development of the first clinical cardiovascular event. We
used data from the Scottish Record Linkage Database to
project forward the long-term consequences of non-fatal
events such as first myocardial infarction, both in terms of
reduced survival and costs of further hospitalisations.

The cost per life-year free from cardiovascular disease
was then calculated, and is shown in Table 2-6. This is presented both as a discounted and non-discounted figure. Discounting is applied both to costs and benefits. The
discounting of costs allows for inflation, but not for any fall
in the price of the drug, which might occur as a result of
competitive pressure or the availability of generic substitutes. Discounting of benefits is used to quantify the fact
that the prevention of an event which would occur, say,
within the next week is more desirable than prevention of
the same event in 5 years' time. The cost-effectiveness of
treatment is not a fixed entity, but is entirely dependent on
he risk level of the subjects selected for therapy. For that
ason, the cost-effectiveness of secondary prevention will
vitably be superior to that of primary prevention (Jons-
et al. 1996; Johannesson et al. 1997). Selection of higher-

ABLE 2-6. Cost-effectiveness of Primary Prevention in WOSCOPS

Treatment Selection	%	Number needed to treat	Cost/LYG £ Undis-counted	Cost/LYG £ Discounted 6%
All WOSCOPS men	100	31.4	8,121	20,375
European Guidelines*	40	22.5	5,601	13,995

* Treatment of subjects at ≥ 10% 5-year risk of CHD death, myocardial infarction, newly diagnosed angina, stroke or transient ischaemic attack (Pyorala et al. 1994).
Cost/LYG=Cost per life-year gained free from cardiovascular disease.
Ref: WOSCOPS Economic analysis (Caro et al. 1997)

risk subjects from the WOSCOPS cohort who would have qualified for treatment according to the European Joint Guidelines (Pyorala et al. 1994) improves the cost-effectiveness in primary prevention as shown in Table 2-6.

Event Reduction Analysis

Influence of baseline lipids on treatment effect

Since the publication of the basic results of WOSCOPS, we have taken the opportunity to undertake additional exploratory analyses in a number of areas. A recently published paper has looked at the relationship between baseline lipid phenotype and clinical outcome on treatment, and at the association of magnitude of lipid changes with event reduction (West of Scotland Coronary Prevention Study Group, 1998b). The baseline levels of LDL and HDL cholesterol and of triglycerides were determined as the mean value of the two pre-randomisation measurements for each of the 6,595 men in the trial. The subjects were then divided into quintiles of baseline lipid level, and the event rates in the placebo and pravastatin treated groups were assessed. Correction was made for baseline covariates using the Cox proportional hazards model. The effect of baseline LDL cholesterol and the effects of treatment are illustrated in Fig 2-2. The association between LDL cholesterol and risk in the placebo group is as expected. It is also clear that pravastatin produced the same relative reduction in risk irrespective of baseline LDL. The same independence between baseline lipid profile and treatment effect was seen in the quintile analysis of HDL and triglycerides.

Relationship between LDL changes and event reduction

In addition to the analysis presented in Fig 2-2, we also investigated the relationship between the reduction in LDL cholesterol and the prevention of events. The on-treatment LDL cholesterol levels were calculated as the mean of all measured values for each individual from the first on-therapy measurement at 6 months onwards till occurrence an event or the end of the trial. Endpoints occurring wit' the first 6 months were excluded from the analysis, s

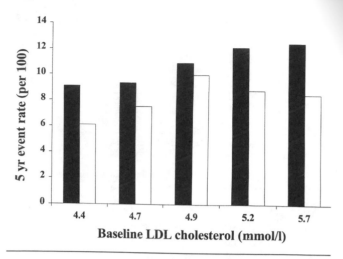

Fig 2-2. Influence of baseline LDL cholesterol on event rate and treat-
ment effect in West of Scotland Coronary Prevention Study Group.
Placebo in solid columns; open columns, pravastatin.
See Reference 42.

no on-treatment LDL levels were available till this time.
The pravastatin-treated subjects were grouped into quintiles
according to the magnitude of LDL reduction from baseline.
The mean reductions in the five quintiles were 0%, 12%,
24%, 31% and 39%. The event rate and relative risk compared with the placebo group were calculated and are dis-
played in Table 7. It should be realised that the majority of
the subjects in the quintile with no mean reduction in LDL
cholesterol had withdrawn from trial medication, and hence
their LDL levels had returned to the pre-treatment (or placebo) values. There may be a small number of genuine non-
responders to pravastatin, but since measurement of drug
levels in plasma or urine is not practicable, it is not possible
to distinguish non-responders from non-compliers.

TABLE 2-7. RELATIONSHIP BETWEEN EXTENT OF LDL
CHOLESTEROL LOWERING AND EVENT REDUCTION IN
WOSCOPS

Quintile	Mean Reduction in LDL Cholesterol		Relative Risk	95% CI
	mmol/l	mg/dl		
1	0	0	1.06	0.81,1.38
2	0.60	23	0.70	0.50,0.96
3	1.16	45	0.57	0.41,0.81
4	1.52	59	0.64	0.47,0.89
5	2.01	78	0.57	0.41,0.78

Relative risk=4.4 year risk of definite or suspect fatal or non-fatal MI, other
cardiovascular death, CABG or PTCA.
Ref: West of Scotland Coronary Prevention Study Group (1998b)

Looking Across the Atlantic: Implications for Guideline Development

US National Cholesterol Education Program

The publication of the results of WOSCOPS, along with the other secondary prevention trials using statins, has provided for the first time an opportunity to validate some of the guidelines on coronary prevention published on both sides of the Atlantic. The Second Report of the Adult Treatment Panel of the National Cholesterol Education Program (NCEP, 1994b) had proposed thresholds for pharmacological lipid lowering based on age and the presence or absence of clinical atherosclerotic disease or of multiple risk factors. The advice on drug treatment was based on the early trials discussed above, plus extrapolation from observational epidemiological studies, particularly Framingham. Table 8 illustrates the thresholds for treatment, and also the proportion of WOSCOPS men who fell into the various categories. Overall, 77% of the WOSCOPS men would have qualified for therapy according to NCEP guidelines. Given the positive results of the study, the recommendations of the NCEP may be seen to be supported by the WOSCOPS results, in indicating that treatment according to the guidelines is safe and effective.

TABLE 2-8. WOSCOPS and the National Cholesterol Education Program Guidelines

Clinical Category	Threshold LDL		Number of WOSCOPS Subjects	%
	mmol/l	mg/dl		
No CHD				
< 2 Risk Factors	≥ 4.9	≥ 190	1 249	18.9
	< 4.9	< 190	1 545	23.4
≥ 2 Risk Factors	≥ 4.1	≥ 160	3 187	48.3
	< 4.1	< 160	0	0
Clinical CHD	≥ 3.4	≥ 130	614	9.3
	< 3.4	< 130	0	0

Joint European Guidelines

In contrast to the NCEP approach, the joint guidelines of the European Societies of Atherosclerosis, Cardiology and Hypertension recommend an explicit estimate of the 10-year risk of developing a major cardiovascular event (CHD death, non-fatal myocardial infarction, stroke or new onset angina pectoris). Individuals whose risk exceeds this threshold despite appropriate lifestyle modification are considered candidates for drug therapy. The more restrictive European guidelines would identify approximately 40% of the WOSCOPS cohort as eligible for treatment. Are the subjects selected for treatment under European guidelines thos greatest risk? We can only answer this question indirectly at present. The European guidelines are based on the Framingham risk equation, which was shown to predict risk successfully in quintiles of the WOSCOPS placebo group. Further analysis on a subject by subject basis will be needed to test the effectiveness of the guidelines more rigorously, but they appear to perform successfully at a first approximation.

British Guidelines

The most stringent guidelines, from the UK Government's Standing Medical Advisory Committee, propose that only patients with a 10-year risk of ≥30% (3% per annum) after other risk factor reduction should be treated with statins (Standing Medical Advisory Committee, 1997). This approach, while clearly the most cost-effective, would result in the smallest proportion of subjects receiving therapy. Significant numbers of events occurring in lower-risk groups would not be prevented by such an approach. For example, if only the top quartile of multivariate risk in WOSCOPS were treated, the group thus selected would have a 5-year risk of fatal CHD or non-fatal infarction of ≥10%, equivalent to a risk of all-cardiovascular events of 15–20% at 5 years, or double that figure at 10 years (West of Scotland Coronary Prevention Study Group, 1997). Treatment restricted to this top quartile would address 45% of all the episodes of fatal CHD or non-fatal infarction, but would leave 55% of all events untreated. The distribution of fatal events is more skewed to the high-risk quartile, in which 59% of fatal CHD occurred.

Summary

The protagonists and antagonists of selective versus inclusive guidelines continue to debate the issue in the correspondence columns of the journals (Reynolds, 1997; Ul Haq et al. 1996; Ramsay et al. 1996; Ul Haq et al. 1995; Garber and Browner, 1997; La Rosa and Pearson, 1997). The nature of the debate reflects the standpoint of the protagonists, with a general tendency for American authorities to advocate a more aggressive approach. This is perhaps to be expected, since much of the concern in Britain relates to the economic impact of implementation of primary prevention with statins within fixed National Health Service (NHS) resources. The "zero sum game" of NHS funding requires the case for primary prevention with statins to be made not in absolute terms, but in competition with existing Health Service priorities. Even when existing treatments in cardiology or other areas may lack the weight of evidence of benefit now available for statins, the process of reallocating resources in the NHS is cumbersome. Under these cost constraints, attempts to prioritise treatment are logical and appropriate, but it should be acknowledged that the process of rationing is based on economic rather than scientific criteria. A further disincentive to widespread use of statins in the NHS relates to the relatively low usage of coronary revascularisation procedures in the UK, and their low unit osts. Under American conditions, for example, the savings in the number and cost of coronary revascularisation procedures by primary prevention goes a long way to offsetting the drug costs, which are no greater in US dollars than in British pounds.

Experience with the introduction of other effective but expensive medical technologies indicates that many of the problems described above will resolve over the next few years. The first of the statin drugs to be marketed, lovastatin, will come off patent protection within the next couple of years, and this is likely to trigger downward pressure on the costs of all drugs in the class. In contrast, the unit costs of myocardial infarction and coronary interventional procedures, which require skilled staff and hospital resources, will continue to increase. These trends will steadily improve the cost-effectiveness of primary prevention with statins, and will result in their increasingly widespread use.

CONCLUSIONS

The results of WOSCOPS and the other statin trials have opened a new era in the primary and secondary prevention of coronary heart disease. Not only have the statins proved to be effective and safe, the trials have contributed to our knowledge of coronary disease, particularly in highlighting the dissociation between regression of atheroma and prevention of coronary events. The concept of plaque stabilisation has emerged as a result of these studies, and is now the target of intensive research effort. The challenge in contemporary preventive cardiology, on both sides of the Atlantic, is to use the new optimism engendered by the statin trials to encourage lifestyle change as well as to use the statins in a logical and cost-effective manner.

ACKNOWLEDGEMENTS

SMC is supported by the British Heart Foundation. The West of Scotland Coronary Prevention Study was undertaken with the support of a research grant from the Bristol-Myers Squibb Company.

REFERENCES

1. Anderson, K.M., Wilson, P.W.F., Odell, P.M. and Kannel, W.B. (1991) An updated coronary risk profile. *Circulation* 83, 357–363.

2. Anonymous (1994a) Randomised trial of cholesterol lowering in 4444 patients with coronary heart disease: the Scandinavian Simvastatin Survival Study (4S). *Lancet* 344, 1383–1389.

3. Anonymous (1994b) National Cholesterol Education Program Second Report of the Expert Panel on Detection, Evaluation, and Treatment of High Blood Cholesterol in Adults (Adult Treatment Panel II). *Circulation* 89, 1333–1445.

4. Assmann, G. and Schulte, H. (1992) Relation of high density lip protein cholesterol and triglycerides to incidence of atherosclerotic coronary artery disease (the PROCAM experience). *American Journal Of Cardiology* 70, 733–737.

5. Buchwald, H., Varco, R.L., Matts, J.P., Long, J.M., Fitch, L.L., Campbell, G.S., Pearce, M.B., Yellin, A.E., Edmiston, W.A., Smink, R.D.J. and et al (1990) Effect of partial ileal bypass surgery on mortality and morbidity from coronary heart disease in patients with hypercholesterolemia. Report of the Program on the Surgical Control of the Hyperlipidemias (POSCH). *New England Journal of Medicine* 323, 946–955.

6. Caro, J., Klittich, W., McGuire, A., Ford, I., Norrie, J., Pettit D, McMurray, J., Shepherd, J. and for the West of Scotland Coronary Prevention Study Group. (1997) The West of Scotland Coronary Prevention Study: economic benefit analysis of primary prevention with pravastatin. *British Medical Journal* 315, 1577–1582.

7. Chen, Z., Peto, R., Collins, R., MacMahon, S., Lu, J. and Li, W. (1991) Serum cholesterol concentration and coronary heart disease in populations with low cholesterol concentrations. *British Medical Journal* 303, 276–282.

8. Committee of Principal Investigators (1984) WHO cooperative trial on primary prevention of ischaemic heart disease with clofibrate to lower serum cholesterol: final mortality follow-up. *Lancet 2*, 600–604.

9. Davey Smith, G. and Pekkanen, J. (1992) Should there be a moratorium on the use of cholesterol lowering drugs? *BMJ* 304, 431–434.

10. Downs, J.R., Clearfield, M., Weiss, S., Whitney, E., Shapiro, D.R., Beere, P.A., Langendorfer, A., Stein, E.A., Kruyer, W., Gotto, A.M.J. for the AFCAPS/TexCAPS Research Group (1998) Extending the benefit: Primary prevention of acute major coronary events with lovastatin in men and women with average cholesterol. Results of the Airforce/Texas Coronary Atherosclerosis Prevention Study (AFCAPS/TexCAPS). *Journal of the American Medical Association.* In press.

11. Frick, M.H., Elo, O., Haapa, K., Heinonen, O.P., Heinsalmi, P., Helo, P., Huttunen, J.K., Kaitaniemi, P., Koskinen, P., Manninen, V. & et al (1987) Helsinki Heart Study: Primary-prevention trial with gemfibrozil in middle-aged men with dyslipidemia. Safety of treatment, changes in risk factors, and incidence of coronary heart disease. *New England Journal of Medicine* 317, 1237–1245.

12. Garber, A.M. and Browner, W.S. (1997) Cholesterol screening guidelines. Consensus, evidence, and common sense. *Circulation* 95, 1642–1645.

13. Gotto, A.M.J. (1997) Cholesterol management in theory and practice. *Circulation* 96, 4424–4430.

14. Gould, A.L., Roussouw, J.E., Santanello, N.C., Heyse, J.F. and Furberg, C.D. (1998) Cholesterol reduction yields clinical benefit. Impact of statin trials. *Circulation* 97, 946–952.

15. Hulley, S.B., Walsh, J.M.B. and Newman, T.B. (1992) Health policy on blood cholesterol: Time to change directions. *Circulation* 86, (pp 1026–1029).

16. Isles, C.G., Hole, D.J., Gillis, C.R., Hawthorne, V.M. and Lever, A.F. (1989) Plasma cholesterol, coronary heart disease, and cancer in the Renfrew and Paisley survey. *BMJ* 298, 920–924.

7. Jacobs, D., Blackburn, H., Higgins, M., Reed, D., Iso, H., McMillan, G., Neaton, J., Nelson, J., Potter, J., Rifkind, B.M., Roussouw, Shekelle, R. and Yusuf, S. (1992) Report of the conference

on low blood cholesterol mortality associations. *Circulation* 86, 1046–1060.

18. Johannesson, M., Jonsson, B., Kjekshus, J., Olsson, A.G., Pedersen, T.R. and Wedel, H. (1997) Cost effectiveness of simvastatin treatment to lower cholesterol levels in patients with coronary heart disease. Scandinavian Simvastatin Survival Study Group. *New England Journal of Medicine* 336, 332–336.

19. Jonsson, B., Johannesson, M., Kjekshus, J., Olsson, A.G., Pedersen, T.R. and Wedel, H. (1996) Cost-effectiveness of cholesterol lowering. Results from the Scandinavian Simvastatin Survival Study (4S). *European Heart Journal* 17, 1001–1007.

20. Keys, A. (1980) Seven Countries: *A Multivariate Analysis of Health and Coronary Heart Disease*. Cambridge, MA: Harvard University Press.

21. La Rosa, J. and Pearson, T.A. (1997) Cholesterol screening guidelines. Consensus, evidence, and the departure from common sense. *Circulation* 95, 1651–1653.

22. La Rosa, J.C., Hunninghake, D., Bush, D., Criqui, M.H., Getz, G.S., Gotto, A.M.J., Grundy, S.M., Rakita, L., Robertson, R.M., Weisfeldt, M.L. et al. (1990) The cholesterol facts. A summary of the evidence relating dietary fats, serum cholesterol, and coronary heart disease. A joint statement by the American Heart Association and the National Heart, Lung, and Blood Institute. The Task Force on Cholesterol Issues, American Heart Association. *Circulation* 81, 1721–1733.

23. Law, M.R., Wald, N.J. and Thompson, S.G. (1996) By how much and how quickly does reduction in serum cholesterol lower risk of ischaemic heart disease? *British Medical Journal* 308, 367–373.

24. Oliver, M.F. (1991) Might treatment of hypercholesterolaemia increase non-cardiac mortality? *Lancet* 337, 1529–1531.

25. Oliver, M.F. (1995) Statins prevent coronary heart disease. *Lancet* 346, 1378–1379.

26. Oliver, M.F., Pyorala, K. and Shepherd, J. (1997) Management of hyperlipidaemia. Why, when and how to treat. *European Heart Journal* 18, 371–375.

27. Peto, R., Yusuf, S. and Collins, R. (1985) Cholesterol lowering trials in their epidemiological context. *Circulation* 72, 451.

28. Pharoah, P.D. and Hollingworth, W. (1996) Cost effectiveness of lowering cholesterol concentration with statins in patients with and without pre-existing coronary heart disease: life table method applied to health authority population. *BMJ* 312, 1443–1448.

29. Pyorala, K., De Backer, G., Graham, I., Poole-Wilson, P. and Wood, D. (1994) Prevention of coronary heart disease in clinical practice. Recommendations of the Task Force of the European Society of Cardiology, European Atherosclerosis Society and European Society of Hypertension. *European Heart Journal* 15, 1300–1331.

30. Ramsay, L.E., Ul Haq, I., Jackson, P.R., Yeo, W.W., Pickin, D.M. and Payne, J.N. (1996) Targeting lipid-lowering drug therapy for primary prevention of coronary disease: an updated Sheffield table. *Lancet* 348, 387–388.

31. Reynolds, T.M. et al. (1997) Use of statins. Standing Medica' Advisory Committee should reconsider advice to use Sheffield ris table [letter]. *BMJ* 315, 1620.

32. Sacks, F.M., Pfeffer, M.A., Moye, L.A., Rouleau, J.L., Ruther J.D., Cole, T.G., Brown, L., Warnica, J.W., Arnold, J.M., Wun Davis, B.R. and Braunwald, E. (1996) The effect of pravas*

coronary events after myocardial infarction in patients with averag‹ cholesterol levels. Cholesterol and Recurrent Events Trial investigators. *New England Journal of Medicine* 335, 1001–1009.

33. Shaper, A.G., Pocock, S.J., Walker, M., Phillips, A.N., Whitehead, T.P. and MacFarlane, P.W. (1985) Risk factors for ischaemic heart disease: the prospective phase of the British Regional Heart Study. *Journal of Epidemiology & Community Health* 39, 197–209.

34. Shepherd, J., Cobbe, S.M., Ford, I., Isles, C.G., Lorimer, A.R., MacFarlane, P.W., McKillop, J.H. and Packard, C.J. (1995) Prevention of coronary heart disease with pravastatin in men with hypercholesterolemia. West of Scotland Coronary Prevention Study Group. *New England Journal of Medicine* 333, 1301–1307.

35. Stamler, J., Wentworth, D. and Neaton, J.D. (1986) Is relationship between serum cholesterol and risk of premature death from coronary heart disease continuous and graded? Findings in 356,222 primary screenees of the Multiple Risk Factor Intervention Trial (MRFIT). *JAMA* 256, 2823–2828.

36. Standing Medical Advisory Committee (1997) The use of statins. *NHS Executive letter EL* (97)44 .

37. The Lipid Research Clinics Coronary Primary Prevention Trial (1984) Results. 1. Reduction in incidence of coronary heart disease. *J Am Med Assoc* 251, 351–364.

38. The West of Scotland Coronary Prevention Study Group. (1992) A coronary primary prevention study of Scottish men aged 45–64 years: trial design. *Journal of Clinical Epidemiology* 45, 849–860.

39. The West of Scotland Coronary Prevention Study Group. (1995) Screening experience and baseline characteristics in the West of Scotland Coronary Prevention Study. *American Journal Of Cardiology* 76, 485–491.

40. The West of Scotland Coronary Prevention Study Group. (1997) Baseline risk factors and their association with outcome in the West of Scotland Coronary Prevention Study. *American Journal of Cardiology* 79, 756–762.

41. The West of Scotland Coronary Prevention Study Group (1998a). Hospitalisation in the West of Scotland Coronary Prevention Study. *Journal of the American College of Cardiology* submitted.

42. The West of Scotland Coronary Prevention Study Group (1998b). Influence of pravastatin and plasma lipids on clinical events in the West of Scotland Coronary Prevention Study. *Circulation* 97, 1440–1445.

43. Tonkin, A. et al (1997) Long Term Intervention with Pravastatin in Ischemic Disease (LIPID). Presented, American Heart Association Annual Scientific Sessions, Orlando, FL.

44. Tunstall-Pedoe, H., Smith, W.C. and Tavendale, R. (1989) How-often-that-high graphs of serum cholesterol. Findings from the Scottish Heart Health and Scottish MONICA studies. *Lancet* 1, 540–542.

45. Ul Haq, I., Jackson, P.R., Yeo, W.W. and Ramsay, L.E. (1995) Sheffield risk and treatment table for cholesterol lowering for primary prevention of coronary heart disease. *Lancet* 346, 1467–1471.

46. Ul Haq, I., Ramsay, L.E., Pickin, D.M., Yeo, W.W., Jackson, P.R. and Payne, J.N. (1996) Lipid-lowering for prevention of coronary heart disease: what policy now? *Clinical Science* 91, 399–413.

7. World Health Organisation European Collaborative Group ?86) European collaborative trial of multifactorial prevention of ›nary heart disease: final report on the 6-year results. *Lancet* 1, ›72.

CHAPTER 3

New Modes of Platelet Inhibition — Is their Application Limited?

Frans Van de Werf

INTRODUCTION

Acute coronary syndromes share a common pathophysiologic mechanism: plaque rupture, fissuring or erosion → platelet activation → thrombus formation. The clinical syndromes that result from disruption of a plaque are: unstable angina pectoris, non-Q wave myocardial infarction and acute transmural myocardial (Q-wave) infarction (Fuster V, 1992). Most cases of transmural myocardial infarction occur as a result of a complete occlusion of the coronary artery (DeWood, 1980). In patients with unstable angina or non-Q wave infarction, massive (transmural) necrosis is prevented because the thrombus is not occlusive, because rapid restoration of flow occurs after a temporary complete occlusion or because of the existence of collateral vessels (DeWood, 1986). At present, aspirin and, to a lesser extent, intravenous heparin are given to nearly all patients with acute coronary syndromes. In patients given thrombolytic therapy with tissue plasminogen activator (t-PA), concomitant, high-dose, intravenous heparin is needed to get the full benefit of this fibrin-specific agent (GUSTO Investigators, 1993). The benefit, if any, of heparin when added to streptokinase is less clear. Overviews of the benefits and risks of subcutaneous or intravenous heparin in patients with suspected acute myocardial infarction have recently been published (Collins, 1996; Ridker, 1993).

Also in studies in patients with unstable angina or non-Q wave myocardial infarction, not receiving thrombolytic agents, the benefit of adding heparin to aspirin is rather limited (RISC Group, 1990; Holdright, 1994). Reactivation of unstable angina and myocardial infarction may occur within hours of the discontinuation of heparin (rebound phenomenon) (Théroux, 1992). Furthermore, activation of the glycoprotein (GP) IIb/IIIa receptors, expression of P-selectin and enhanced platelet aggregation were recently demonstrated at therapeutic concentrations of heparin in patients with unstable angina (Xiao and Théroux, 1998). Thus, aspirin clearly is the key antithrombotic agent for the treatment of all patients with acute coronary syndromes, whereas the benefit of heparin is less striking.

Significant benefit of aspirin is evident not only among patients with acute coronary syndromes but also among patients with a past history of myocardial infarction, stroke, or transient ischemic attack and among patients with stable angina or peripheral vascular disease (Antiplatelet Trialists' Collaboration, 1994). Reductions in vascular events of about 25% were observed with aspirin alone in a total of 45,000 patients studied in 46 trials of secondary prevention.

LIMITATIONS OF ASPIRIN

In spite of being very effective, aspirin has several limitations. Aspirin is a relatively weak antiplatelet agent. It inactivates prostaglandin G/H synthase resulting in a permanent and irreversible loss of cyclo-oxygenase activity (Patrono, 1994). Loss of cyclo-oxygenase activity ultimately results in decreased formation of eicosanoids including thromboxane A_2, a potent agonist of platelet aggregation and vasoconstrictor. Blockade of thromboxane A_2, however, will not prevent platelet aggregation via other, thromboxane A_2-independent, pathways (Fig 3-1). Furthermore, cyclo-oxygenase activity is also required for the generation of antithrombotic prostaglandins by endothelial cells such as prostacyclin which is a potent endogenous platelet inhibitor and vasodilator. In addition, aspirin, even in low doses, may be associated with gastrointestinal side effects and may induce severe bronchospasm in allergic patients.

Platelet activation

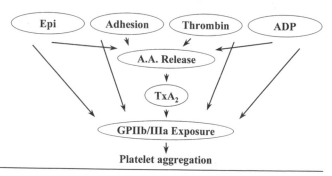

Figure 3-1 : *Schematic and simplified representation of pathways of platelet activation. AA: arachidonic acid; ADP: adenosine diphosphate; TxA_2: thromboxane A_2; epi: epinephrine.*

NEW ANTIPLATELET AGENTS

Many new, more potent antiplatelet agents such as thromboxane synthase inhibitors, antagonists of the adenosine diphosphate (ADP), serotonin-, endoperoxide- and GP IIb/IIIa-receptors are now available for clinical evaluation in patients with coronary artery disease. The best tested and most promising agents so far are the inhibitors of the GPIIb/IIIa receptor. These receptors belong to the integrin family and bind fibrinogen and other adhesive proteins such as fibronectin, vitronectin and von Willebrand factor to form cross-bridges between adjacent platelets (Lefkovits, 1995). The GPIIb/IIIa receptor recognizes an Arg-Gly-Asp (RGD) sequence (in several adhesive proteins) as well as a Lys-Gln-Ala-Gly-Asp-Val sequence (in fibrinogen). These molecular interactions constitute the final common pathway of platelet aggregation, irrespective of the stimulus (agonist) (Fig 3-1).

In recent years antagonists of the GPIIb/IIIa-receptor have been evaluated in patients undergoing coronary interventions and in patients with unstable coronary syndromes. Monoclonal antibodies with specific activity against the GPIIb/IIIa receptor were the first agents developed. c7E3, a chimeric monoclonal antibody Fab fragment, now called abciximab, has already undergone extensive clinical evaluation, especially during coronary interventions. Other GPIIb/IIIa antagonists are based on the RGD sequence (RGD "mimetics"), representing the "adhesive sequence" in several adhesive proteins such as fibrinogen, fibronectin, von Willebrand factor and vitronectin. Natural RGD-containing peptides have been isolated from the venom of vipers. Integrilin (eptifibatide) is a synthetic cyclic peptide in which the Arg component has been substituted by Lys (KGD). Synthetic, peptidomimetic antagonists such as lamifiban and tirofiban were designed to avert some of the problems of peptides including instability and a short survival in the circulation. Orally-active inhibitors of the GPIIb/IIIa receptor have been developed. They are inherently orally active or they are metabolized to the active form after ingestion (e.g. orbofiban, xemilofiban, sibrafiban, lefradafiban, klerval, SB 21 4857).

Although GPIIb/IIIa receptor agonists are very promising new agents to control platelet function, other agents have interesting properties as well. For example, ticlopidine and clopidogrel are selective antagonists of ADP-induced platelet aggregation (Schrör, 1993). They also reduce responses to other agonists which require feedback amplification by ADP release and inhibit the GPIIb/IIIa-fibrinogen interaction triggered by ADP.

Despite theoretical advantages, selective inhibitors of thromboxane synthase have failed to show superiority over aspirin in animal studies probably due to the accumulation of PG-endoperoxide intermediates that can act as antagonists of the thromboxane A_2 receptors. To circumvent this problem combined thromboxane A_2 synthase inhibitor and thromboxane A_2 receptor blockers have been developed. Ridogrel is such an agent (De Clerck, 1989). It has been tested as an adjunct to thrombolysis in 907 patients with acute myocardial infarction with streptokinase (the Ridogrel versus Aspirin Patency Trial, RAPT) (RAPT investigators, 1994). In this setting, the coronary artery patency results were slightly disappointing but a reduced incidence of ischemic events during hospital stay and, also, a significant mortality reduction at one year (unpublished data) were observed with ridogrel as compared to aspirin. Further development of this agent has been stopped. Other thromboxane synthase inhibitors and receptor antagonists have not come to full clinical investigation.

USE OF NEW PLATELET ANTAGONISTS IN CORONARY INTERVENTIONS

The present experience with intravenous administration of GPIIb/IIIa receptor antagonists is summarized in Table 3-1.

The Evaluation of c7E3 in Preventing Ischemic Complications (EPIC) trial was the first large trial showing a reduction in ischemic/thrombotic events following angioplasty and other interventions with a GPIIb/IIIa antagonist in high-risk patients, however, at the cost of an increased risk of bleeding complications (EPIC Investigators, 1994). Most major bleeding complications in EPIC occurred at the femoral access site and were more often seen in elderly patients and in women, especially after complex procedures (Aguirre, 1995). Surprisingly, this trial also demonstrated a significant reduction in recurrent ischemic events up to six months following the procedure (Topol, 1994). Recently, two other large studies with abciximab in patients undergoing coronary interventions have been prematurely stopped because of a highly significant reduction in the primary composite endpoint of the trial (death, myocardial infarction or need for urgent intervention) in the group receiving abciximab. It is unusual in the field of acute coronary syndromes and coronary interventions that a trial is stopped prematurely because of clinical efficacy (Van de Werf, 1996). In the EPILOG (Evaluation of PTCA to Improve Long-term Outcome by c7E3 Glycoprotein receptor blockade) trial a total of 2,980 patients undergoing elective angioplasty were to be randomized between standard therapy with placebo, abciximab with low-dose heparin or abciximab with standard-dose heparin (EPILOG Investigators, 1997). After the first interim analysis a highly signifi-

TABLE 3-1: CURRENT CLINICAL EXPERIENCE WITH INTRAVENOUS GPIIB/IIIA ANTAGONISTS

	Angioplasty	Stent	UA/NQWMI	ST ↑ AMI
Abciximab	EPIC[9] EPILOG[10] CAPTURE[4] RAPPORT[40]	EPISTENT[41]	—	TAMI-8[18] TIMI-14[38] SPEED* RAPPORT[40]
Integrilin	IMPACT-II[16]	—	PURSUIT[27]	IMPACT-MI[22] Ronner A. et al.[32]
Lamifiban	—	—	PARAGON[23]	PARADIGM[21]
Tirofiban	RESTORE[29]	—	PRISM[26] PRISM-PLUS[25]	—

UA: unstable angina; NQWMI: non-Q wave myocardial infarction; ST ↑ AMI: ST-segment elevation acute myocardial infarction.
* Data not yet presented.

cant reduction in the primary endpoint was observed in patients receiving abciximab. An excess of major bleeding complications was found in the abciximab with high-dose heparin group but not in the abciximab plus low-dose heparin group. In the CAPTURE trial (a phase III randomized, placebo-controlled multicenter trial of c7E3 in patients scheduled for urgent PTCA due to refractory unstable angina), 1,400 patients with refractory unstable angina were to be randomized between placebo or abciximab (in addition to standard treatment) during 16 to 24 h preceding angioplasty and continuing one hour following the completion of the procedure. The interim analysis in 1,050 patients also showed a highly significant reduction in the composite endpoint of death, myocardial infarction or need for urgent intervention in the abciximab group (CAPTURE Investigators, 1997). A non-significant increase in major bleeding complications with abciximab was also found in this trial. The key results of EPIC, EPILOG and CAPTURE are summarized in table 3-2 and clearly indicate that abciximab is able to reduce the risk of thrombotic/ ischemic complications following coronary interventions. The use of abciximab in this setting is associated with an increased risk of bleeding complications. This increased risk is partly due to the concomitant administration of heparin. The EPILOG data show that lowering the dose of heparin together with early vascular sheath removal reduce the excess of bleeding complications with abciximab. Recently, the positive effect of abciximab in coronary interventions has been extended to primary PTCA and elective stenting. In the RAPPORT trial the administration of abciximab during primary PTCA for acute myocardial infarction has been studied in 483 patients (Topol, 1997). There was a 48% reduction in the composite endpoint of death, reinfarction or urgent reintervention at 30 days and a 38% reduction at 6 months in the PTCA plus abciximab group vs the PTCA alone group. In the EPILOG Stent study — also called the EPISTENT — 2,399 patients were randomized between stent implantation alone, stent implantation plus abciximab and PTCA plus abciximab. Statistically significant reductions in the composite endpoint of death, myocardial infarction and urgent revascularization at 30 days were found in the two groups receiving abciximab (5.3% and 6.9% for stent plus abciximab and PTCA plus abciximab, respec-

TABLE 3-2: ABCIXIMAB IN CORONARY ANGIOPLASTY: 30-DAY COMPOSITE ENDPOINT OF DEATH, MYOCARDIAL INFARCTION OR REPEAT INTERVENTION IN PATIENTS UNDERGOING CORONARY INTERVENTION

	Placebo	Abciximab (bolus + infusion)	Reduction	P
EPIC[9] n=2,099	12.8 %	8.3 %	35 %	0.008
CAPTURE[4] n=1,265	15.4 %	11.3 %	27 %	0.012
EPILOG[10] n=2,792	11.7 %	5.3 %	54 %	0.0001

tively vs 10.8% in the stent alone group). No abrupt closures occurred in the stent plus abciximab group whereas 6 cases were observed in the stent alone and 4 cases in the PTCA plus abciximab group (Topol, 1998). Taken together, these recent data further support the use of abciximab for all types of coronary interventions.

Eptifibatide (integrilin) and tirofiban have also been studied in patients undergoing coronary interventions. Two large trials have been reported: the IMPACT II (Integrilin to Minimize the Platelet Aggregation and prevent Coronary Thrombosis) (IMPACT II Investigators, 1997) and the RESTORE (Randomized Efficacy Study of Tirofiban for Outcomes and REstenosis) (RESTORE Investigators, 1997) trial. Although both trials failed to show a significant reduction in their primary endpoint, the overall results are concordant with those observed in the trials with abciximab. During the infusion of integrilin (eptifibatide) and tirofiban significant reductions in both the incidence of subsequent myocardial infarction and the need for repeat angioplasty were found. Several reasons have been put forward to explain the less convincing results obtained with the non-antibody GPIIb/IIIa inhibitors. First, there are animal data suggesting that RGD-mimetics may act as partial agonists and, therefore, are less effective. Other explanations could be the absence of inhibition of the vitronectin receptor that shares the same beta unit as the GPIIb/IIIa receptors and the shorter half-life and the relatively weak affinity for the GPIIb/IIIa receptor as compared with abciximab.

The combination of aspirin plus ticlopidine has been shown to be very effective in preventing thrombotic complications after stent deployment (Schömig, 1996). In 257 patients highly significant reductions in the risk of myocardial infarction, repeated intervention and hemorrhagic and vascular complications were observed in patients randomized to the combination aspirin plus ticlopidine vs conventional anticoagulant therapy. These results were confirmed by a much larger study in about 1,500 patients (STARS study) (Leon, 1996).

Synergistic and accelerated platelet inhibitory effects of the combination ticlopidine and aspirin, recently demonstrated in patients after stent deployment (Rupprecht HJ, 1998), may be an explanation for the excellent results observed in patients after stent implantation.

UNSTABLE ANGINA AND NON-Q WAVE INFARCTION

Integrilin (eptifibatide), lamifiban and tirofiban have also been tested in large-scale phase III trials in patients with unstable angina/non-Q wave myocardial infarction: PURSUIT (Platelet IIb/IIIa in Unstable angina: Receptor Suppression Using Integrilin Therapy), Platelet IIb/IIIa Antagonist for the Reduction of Acute coronary syndrome events in a Global Organization Network (PARAGON); and latelet Receptor Inhibition for ischemic Syndrome Management (PRISM) and Platelet Receptor Inhibition for ischemic Syndrome Management in Patients Limited by Unstable Signs and symptoms (PRISM plus), respectively (Table 3-3).

The PARAGON trial was the first reported (PARAGON Investigators, 1996). In the first phase of PARAGON (called PARAGON A) patients with acute coronary syndromes were randomized to two doses of lamifiban (300 µg bolus + 1 µg/min. or 750 µg bolus + 5 µg/min.) with or without APTT-adjusted intravenous heparin or to placebo plus heparin. All patients were given oral aspirin. The primary endpoint of the trial was death or (re)infarction at 30 days. Only minor differences in the incidence of this endpoint were observed among the 5 treatment groups: 10.8% for low-dose lamifiban without heparin, 10.3% for low-dose lamifiban with heparin, 11.6% for high-dose lamifiban without heparin, 12.3% for high-dose lamifiban plus heparin and 11.7% for placebo plus heparin. These results were unexpected and very much a surprise for the investigators. An even bigger surprise were the long-term results of PARAGON A: at 6 months a significant 28% odds reduction for death or (re)infarction was observed with the low-dose lamifiban group. The reason for the disappointing results of PARAGON A at 30 days are unknown. It is possible that the two selected doses of lamifiban were either too low or too high. A *post hoc* analysis of the PARAGON A data indicates that plasma concentrations of lamifiban and receptor occupancy in PARAGON A are critically dependent on renal function and that with a steady state concentration of 18-42 ng/ml a 40% reduction in death and myocardial infarction was obtained (B. Steiner, personal communication). It is remarkable that the high dose of lamifiban as used in PARAGON A, was not only associated with an increase in major bleeding complications but also with a lower efficacy as compared with the low dose. This raises the possibility that high doses of antithrombotic agents may be harmful in acute coronary syndromes due to the induction of a plaque hemorrhage, which may further increase the mechanical obstruction induced by the culprit lesion. There is also the possibility that spontaneous rupture or erosion of a plaque in unstable coronary syndromes represents a less severe stimulus for platelet aggregation than vessel injury due to angioplasty, hence the failure of more potent antiplatelet agents to yield similarly good results as in patients undergoing coronary interventions. Finally, the PARAGON A study was clearly underpowered to find significant differences in clinical endpoints.

In the PRISM trial patients with unstable angina or non-Q wave myocardial infarction were randomized to tirofiban (n=1,616) or heparin (n=1,616). This study represents the first large trial of an intravenous GPIIb/IIIa inhibitor not used on a background of heparin (PRISM Study Investigators, 1998). All patients received aspirin. The primary endpoint, namely the composite occurrence of death, (re)infarction or refractory ischemia, was at the end of the study drug infusion (48 hrs). A significant 33% risk reduction for this primary endpoint at 48 hrs was observed with tirofiban. At 30 days (3.8% vs 5.6%) the results for the composite

TABLE 3-3: Design of the Phase III Trials with Intravenous GPIIb/IIIa Inhibitors in Patients with Acute Coronary Syndromes

Study name	GPIIb/IIIa Inhibitor	Control group	Study endpoint
PARAGON A[23]	Lamifiban in 2 doses With or without heparin	aspirin + heparin	death plus MI at 30 days
PURSUIT[27]	Integrilin in 2 doses* With heparin	aspirin + heparin	death plus MI at 30 days
PRISM[26]	Tirofiban without heparin	aspirin + heparin	death plus MI plus refractory ischemia at 48 hours
PRISM plus[25]	Tirofiban with and without heparin*	aspirin + heparin	death plus MI plus refractory ischemia at 7 days

* one arm prematurely stopped

endpoint favored tirofiban (15.9 vs 17.1%) but they were not statistically different. A significant (38%) risk reduction for death alone was maintained at 30 days (2.3% vs 3.6%).

In PRISM-plus, patients with unstable angina and non-Q wave myocardial infarction at higher risk (documented ST-T changes on admission) were randomized to receive tirofiban (same dose as in PRISM), heparin or a combination of tirofiban (at a lower dose) plus heparin (PRISM-plus Study Investigators, 1998). The primary endpoint of the study was the incidence of the composite of death, (re)infarction or refractory ischemia within 7 days. At the time of the first unblinded interim analysis the DSMB recommended the tirofiban alone arm of the study because of an excess mortality seen at 7 days. The trial continued in a blinded fashion enrolling 773 patients to the combination tirofiban plus heparin and 797 patients to heparin alone. At 7 days a significant 32% reduction for the primary composite endpoint was found with tirofiban plus heparin 12.9% vs 17.9 for heparin alone.

At 30 days the difference between the two groups remained significant for this composite endpoint (18.5% vs 22.3%, p=0.039). A pooled analysis of the mortality data from the corresponding cohorts in PRISM and PRISM-plus did not show statistical evidence for an excess mortality with tirofiban alone as compared with heparin. Overall outcomes with tirofiban alone including death, (re)infarction rate, recurrent ischemia and the composite endpoint were similar to those with heparin alone.

In the PURSUIT trial, the largest trial performed with an intravenous GPIIb/IIIa receptor antagonist, patients were randomized between placebo and two doses of integrilin (eptifibatide) (PURSUIT Investigators, 1998). After a first interim analysis the low-dose integrilin arm was dropped and randomization continued between placebo (n=4,739) and high-dose integrilin (n=4,722). All patients received aspirin and heparin. A statistically significant 1.5% absolute reduction in the incidence of death or (re)infarction at 30 days was observed in the integrilin group (14.2% vs 15.7%) but at the cost of an increase in bleeding complications and an increased rate of transfusion. However, an equally low incidence of intracranial hemorrhage was observed in both treatment groups.

The key results of the "4P" trials for the endpoint of death or (re)infarction at 30 days are summarized in figure 2. A highly significant, absolute risk reduction of 1.6% was observed favoring the GPIIb/IIIa antagonists.

A large scale trial with another new antiplatelet agent, clopidogrel in ±9,000 patients with acute coronary syndromes is being planned as well (OASIS-4).

GPIIb/IIIa INHIBITORS IN ACUTE MYOCARDIAL INFARCTION

Four trials have studied the use of GPIIb/IIIa inhibitors as adjunct to a full-dose thrombolytic: the eighth Thrombolysis

30 Day Death or Nonfatal Myocardial Infarction

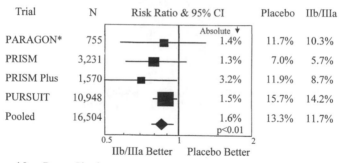

Trial	N	Risk Ratio & 95% CI	Placebo	IIb/IIIa
PARAGON*	755	Absolute 1.4%	11.7%	10.3%
PRISM	3,231	1.3%	7.0%	5.7%
PRISM Plus	1,570	3.2%	11.9%	8.7%
PURSUIT	10,948	1.5%	15.7%	14.2%
Pooled	16,504	1.6% p<0.01	13.3%	11.7%

0.5   1   2
IIb/IIIa Better   Placebo Better

* Low Dose vs Placebo

Figure 3-2 : Meta-analysis of the "4P" trials for the combined endpoint of death or nonfatal myocardial infarction at 30 days, in patients with acute coronary syndromes.

and Myocardial Infarction (TAMI-8) trial (Kleiman, 1993), the Integrilin to Minimize Platelet Aggregation and prevent Coronary Thrombosis — Acute Myocardial Infarction (IMPACT-AMI) (Ohman EM, 1997), Platelet Aggregation Receptor Antagonist Dose Investigation for reperfusion Gain in Myocardial infarction (PARADIGM) (Moliterno DJ, 1996) and a trial with integrilin (eptifibatide) and streptokinase (Ronner, 1998). The results of these relatively small trials did not show very striking results although they all suggest, directly or indirectly, improved reperfusion with the GPIIb/IIIa inhibitor. Two much larger angiographic studies with a reduced dose of a thrombolytic and full-dose abciximab are under way (TIMI-14 and SPEED). Preliminary data from TIMI-14 suggest that with 50 mg tPA over 60 min. in combination with abciximab TIMI 3 flow can be obtained in 75% to 80% of the patients (TIMI-14 Investigators, 1998). It is noteworthy that the experience with a combination of a GPIIb/IIIa inhibitor and streptokinase has not been very positive in the various trials. Either a limited improvement in TIMI flow (Moliterno, 1996; Ronner, 1998) or a high incidence of bleeding complications (TIMI-14 Investigators, 1998; Ronner et al, 1998) has been observed. Conversely, encouraging results have been found with direct antithrombins in combination with streptokinase as compared with tPA (White, 1997; GUSTO-IIb Investigators, 1996).

SECONDARY PREVENTION

Aspirin is well accepted for the secondary prevention of ischemic heart disease (Antiplatelet Trialists' Collaboration, 1994). Important reductions in the incidence of death, (re)infarction and other ischemic events such as stroke have been documented in patients with atherosclerosis. The first large phase III study in secondary prevention with a new antiplatelet agent, Clopidogrel versus Aspirin in Patients at Risk of Ischemic Events (CAPRIE), has recently been published (CAPRIE Steering Committee, 1996). At least 6,300 patients in each of three clinical subgroups (recent ischemic stroke, recent myocardial infarction and peripheral arterial disease) were randomized and followed for a maximum of three years. A modest reduction (8.7%) in the combined risk of ischemic stroke, myocardial infarction or vascular death was observed in the total study population. The greatest benefit was found in the group with peripheral arterial disease. Side effects such as bleeding complications did not occur more often with clopidogrel indicating that this agent is a safe alternative to aspirin.

Secondary prevention trials with oral GPIIb/IIIa antagonists in high-risk, post acute coronary syndrome patients are ongoing (e.g. SYMPHONY with sibrafiban, OPUS with orbofiban) or are being planned (BRAVO with SB 21 4857, Phase III program with klerval). If these studies would show a benefit over aspirin, studies in patients at low risk but with proven coronary artery disease will follow.

Conclusions and Future Directions

It is very likely that our current antithrombotic therapy in acute coronary syndromes (aspirin and heparin) will be replaced by more effective agents in the near future. GPIIb/IIIa receptor antagonists are, at present, the most promising antiplatelet agents. Whether these agents will be more effective and safer than aspirin for secondary prevention remains to be evaluated in well-controlled clinical studies. Presently, these agents have clearly shown to be superior to standard treatment in the setting of coronary interventions. The results of the "4P" trials indicate that these agents have also a future for the acute phase treatment of unstable coronary syndromes. Large trials with orally-active GPIIb/IIIa receptor antagonists are needed in order to test the hypothesis that prolonged, partial, inhibition of the GPIIb/IIIa receptor is better than aspirin (alone) for secondary prevention after an acute coronary syndrome. These trials are under way. Whether these agents have a future for secondary prevention in all patients with proven (coronary) atherosclerosis remains to be seen.

In conclusion, if new modes of platelet inhibition will prove to be more effective and at least as safe as aspirin there should be no limit to their application in all types of patients with proven atherosclerosis provided the costs of these new medications are reasonable.

References

1. Agruirre FV, Topol E, Furguson JJ, Anderson K, Blankenship JC, Heuser RR, Sigmon K, Taylor M, Gottlieb R, Hanovich G, Rosenberg M, Donohue TJ, Weisman HF, Califf RM. Bleeding complications with the chimeric antibody to platelet GPIIb/IIIa integrin in patients undergoing percutaneous coronary intervention. *Circulation* 1995; 91: 2882–2890.

2. Antiplatelet Trialists' Collaboration. Collaborative overview of randomized trials of antiplatelet therapy — I: prevention of death, myocardial infarction, and stroke by prolonged antiplatelet therapy in various categories of patients. *Br Med J* 1994; 308: 81–106.

3. CAPRIE Steering Committee. A randomized, blinded trial of clopidogrel versus aspirin in patients at risk of ischemic events (CAPRIE). *Lancet* 1996; 348: 1329–1338.

4. CAPTURE Investigators. Randomized placebo-controlled trial of abciximab before and during coronary intervention in refractory unstable angina: the CAPTURE study. *Lancet* 1997; 349:1429–1435.

5. Collins R, Mac Mahon S, Flather M et al. Clinical effects of anticoagulant therapy in suspected acute myocardial infarction: systematic overview of randomised trials. *Br Med J* 1996; 313: 652–659.

6. De Clerck F, Beertens J, De Chaffoy de Courcelles D, Freyne E, Janssen PAJ. R68070: Thromboxane A2 synthetase inhibition and thromboxane A2/prostaglandin endoperoxide receptor blockade combined in one molecule. I. Biochemical profile in vitro. *Thromb Haemostas* 1989; 61: 35–42.

7. DeWood MA, Spores J, Notske R, Mouser LT, Burroughs R, Golden MS, Lang HT. Prevalence of total coronary occlusion during the early hours of transmural myocardial infarction. *N Engl J Med* 1980; 303: 897–902.

8. DeWood MA, Stifter WF, Simpson CA, Spores J, Eugster GS, Judge TP, Hinnen ML. Coronary arteriographic findings soon after non-Q-wave myocardial infarction. *N Engl J Med* 1986; 315: 417–423.

9. EPIC Investigators. Use of a monoclonal antibody directed against the platelet glycoprotein IIb/IIIa receptor in high-risk coronary angioplasty. *N Engl J Med* 1994; 330: 956–61.

10. EPILOG Investigators. Effect of platelet glycoprotein IIb/IIIa receptor inhibitor, abciximab, with lower heparin dosages on ischemic complications of percutaneous coronary revascularization. *N Engl J Med* 1997; 336: 1689–1696.

11. Fuster V, Badimon L, Badimon JJ, et al. The pathogenesis of coronary artery disease and the acute coronary syndromes (1). *N Engl J Med* 1992; 326: 242–250.

12. Fuster V, Badimon L, Badimon JJ, et al. The pathogenesis of coronary artery disease and the acute coronary syndromes (2). *N Engl J Med* 1992; 326: 310–318.

13. GUSTO Investigators. An international randomized trial comparing four thrombolytic strategies for acute myocardial infarction. *N Engl J Med* 1993; 329: 673–682.

14. GUSTO IIb Investigators. A comparison of recombinant hirudin and heparin for the treatment of acute coronary syndromes. *N Engl J Med* 1996; 335: 775–782.

15. Holdright D, Patel D, Cunningham D et al. Comparison of the effect of heparin and aspirin versus aspirin alone on transient myocardial ischemia and in-hospital prognosis in patients with unstable angina. *J Am Coll Cardiol* 1994; 24: 39–45.

16. IMPACT II Investigators. Randomized placebo-controlled trial of effect of eptifibatide on complications of percutaneous coronary intervention. *Lancet* 1997; 349:1422–1428.

17. King SB III. Administration of tirofiban (MK-0383) will reduce the incidence of adverse cardiac outcome following PTCA/DCA (RESTORE). *J Am Coll Cardiol* 1996; 27 (suppl A): xxi.

18. Kleiman NS, Ohman ME, Califf RM, et al. Profound inhibition of platelet aggregation with monoclonal antibody 7E3 Fab following thrombolytic therapy: results of the TAMI 8 pilot study. *J Am Coll Cardiol* 1993; 22: 381–389.

19. Lefkovits J, Plow EF, Topol EJ. Platelet glycoprotein IIb/IIIa receptors in cardiovascular medicine. *N Engl J Med* 1995; 332: 1553–1559.

20. Leon MB, Baim DS, Gordon P et al. Clinical and angiographic results from the stent anticoagulation regimen study (STARS). *Circulation* 1996; 94 (suppl I): I-685.

21. Moliterno DJ, Harrington RA, Krucoff MW, et al. More complete and stable reperfusion with platelet IIb/IIIa antagonism plus thrombolysis for AMI: the PARADIGM trial. *Circulation* 1996; 94: 3232. Abstract.

22. Ohman EM, Kleiman NS, Gracioch G, et al. Combined accelerated tissue-plasminogen activator and platelet glycoprotein IIb/IIIa integrin receptor blockade with Integrilin in acute myocardial infarction. *Circulation* 1997; 95: 846–854.

23. PARAGON Investigators. A randomized trial off potent platelet IIb/IIIa antagonism, heparin or both in patients with unstable angina: the PARAGON Study. *Circulation* 1996, 94:I–553.

24. Patrono C. Aspirin as an antiplatelet drug. *N Engl J Med* 1994; 330: 1287–1294.

25. PRISM-plus Study Investigators: Inhibition of the platelet glycoprotein IIb/IIIa receptor with tirofiban in unstable angina and non-Q wave myocardial infarction. *New Engl J Med* 1998; 338:1488–1497.

26. PRISM Study Investigators: A comparison of aspirin plus tirofiban with aspirin plus heparin for unstable angina. *New Engl J Med* 1998; 338:1498–1505.

27. PURSUIT Investigators: The PURSUIT Study. Presented at the XIXth congress of the European Society of Cardiology, in Stockholm, August, 1997.

28. RAPT investigators : Randomized Trial of Ridogrel, a Combined Thromboxane A_2 Synthase Inhibitor and Thromboxane A_2/ Prostaglandin Endoperoxide Receptor Antagonist, Versus Aspirin as Adjunct to Thrombolysis in Patients With Acute Myocardial Infarction. The Ridogrel Versus Aspirin Patency Trial (RAPT). *Circulation* 1994; 89; 588–595.

29. RESTORE Investigators. Effects of platelet glycoprotein IIb/IIIa blockade with tirofiban on adverse cardiac events in patients with unstable angina or acute myocardial infarction undergoing coronary angioplasty. *Circulation* 1997; 96: 1445–1453.

30. Ridker PM, Hebert PR, Fuster V, Henneken CH. Are both aspirin and heparin justified as adjuncts to thrombolytic therapy for acute myocardial infarction? *Lancet* 1993; 341: 1574–1577.

31. RISC Group. Risk of myocardial infarction and death during treatment with low dose aspirin and heparin in men with unstable coronary artery disease. *Lancet* 1990; 336:827–830.

32. Ronner A, van Kesteren HAM, Zijnen P et al. Combined therapy with Streptokinase and Integrilin. *J Am Coll Cardiol* 1998; 31 (suppl A): 191A.

33. Rupprecht HJ, Darius H, Borkowski U et al. Comparison of antiplatelet effects of aspirin, ticlopidine or their combination after stent implantation. *Circulation* 1998; 97:1046–1052.

34. Schömig A, Neumann FJ, Kastrati A, et al. A randomized comparison of antiplatelet and anticoagulant therapy after the placement of coronary stents. *N Engl J Med* 1996; 334:1084-1089.

35. Schrör K. The basic pharmacology of ticlopidine and clopidogrel. *Platelets* 1993; 4:252–61.

36. Tcheng JE, Lincoff AM, Sigmon KN, Kitt MM, Califf RM, Topol EJ for the IMPACT II Investigators. Platelet glycoprotein IIb/IIIa inhibition with integrilin during percutaneous coronary intervention: the IMPACT II Trial. *Circulation* 1995; 92 (suppl): I-543.

37. Théroux P, Waters D, Lam J, Juneau M, McCans J. Reactivation of unstable angina after discontinuation of heparin. *N Engl J Med* 1992; 327: 141–145.

38. TIMI 14 Investigators. The TIMI14 Study. Presented at the Scientific Sessions of the American College of Cardiology in Atlanta, March 1998.

39. Topol EJ, Califf RM, Weisman HF, Ellis SG, Tcheng JE, Worley S, Ivanhoe R, George BS, Fintel D, Weston M, et al. Randomised trial of coronary intervention with antibody against platelet IIb/IIIa integrin for reduction of clinical restenosis: results at six months. The EPIC Investigators. *Lancet* 1994; 343: 881–6.

40. Topol EJ. ReoPro in acute myocardial infarction and primary PTCA organization and randomization trial (RAPPORT). Presented at the XIXth congress of the European Society of Cardiology, in Stockholm, August, 1997.

41. Topol EJ. The EPISTENT study. Presented at the Scientific Sessions of the American College of Cardiology in Atlanta, March 1998.

42. Van de Werf F. More evidence for a beneficial effect of platelet glycoprotein IIb/IIIa blockade during coronary interventions. Latest results from the EPILOG and CAPTURE trials. *Eur Heart J* 1996; 17: 325–326.

43. White HD, Aylward PE, Frey MJ et al. Randomized double-blind comparison of hirulog vs heparin in patients receiving streptokinase and aspirin for acute myocardial infarction (HERO). *Circulation* 1997; 96: 2155–2161.

44. Xiao Z and Théroux P. Platelet activation with unfractionated heparin at therapeutic concentrations and comparisons with a low-molecular-weight heparin and with a direct thrombin inhibitor. *Circulation* 1998; 97: 251–256.

CHAPTER 4

Cardiac nutrition and anti-oxidants: Where are the limits?

Morris Brown

INTRODUCTION

We all know that nutrition plays a major role in the genesis of ischaemic heart disease. Yet a cursory look at the data (were such possible) would show how complex the links must be, and the proof of cause-and-effect relationship by prospective trials is absent for most nutrients. Both for our understanding of ischaemic heart disease, and for its prevention, the complexity is a serious problem. For instance, transgenic models of disease are now often excellent proofs of concept for single disease factors, but a minefield when several factors interact. And moving from mice to men, it is difficult to persuade the majority of a population to alter their diet when it is plain that the majority are unlikely to benefit from such a change.

Similar comments pertain to the genetic basis of ischaemic heart disease. We all know again that some families are more affected than others. But instances where a single gene mutation clearly results in ischaemic heart disease are rare; even mutations of the LDL receptor are not certain to cause disease unless the patient is the one-in-a-million homozygote. In several of the common, complex human disorders — diabetes, asthma, hypertension — genetic studies have found favour as an apparently exact science that will provide some of the missing answers re causation. Ischaemic heart disease however suffers from being not only the end result of numerous, interacting processes, but itself a mixture of stable, unstable and thrombotic processes that are likely to vary in relative importance among patients. The high prevalence of ischaemic heart disease also makes it the most difficult in which to investigate the genetic basis since contributing genetic variants will be common in both healthy and affected subjects; the maximum possible differences between observed and expected frequencies are small, effectively ruling out linkage studies and bedevilling interpretation of associations (like that with the ACE gene deletion polymorphism).

The thesis of this paper will be that greater progress in prevention and understanding of ischaemic heart disease might be achieved by setting limits to the art of the possible. That in prevention, it is more realistic to expect compliance with blandishments to increase dietary intake or add a vitamin pill (as evidenced by the success of the nutriceutical trade), than with injunctions to reduce certain dietary intake. And in genetics, the detection and incrimination of functional variants will advance most easily by targeting discrete biochemical reactions where genotype-phenotype correlations are easily measured. The obvious link between these programmes of prevention and understanding is the study of pathways where a vitamin plays direct or indirect role of co-factor, where we hypothesise that genetic variants reduce affinity — and therefore increase requirement — for that vitamin. Two systems will be described where a mixture of circumstantial and prospective data now exists. The first is endothelial nitric oxide synthase (eNOS), with the possibility that α tocopherol will compensate for reduced production by protecting nitric oxide (NO) from oxidative destruction. The second system centres on homocysteine, and the various B vitamin dependent enzymes by which it is metabolised. Most excitingly, but presently quite speculative, is the potential link between these two systems provided by a little known pathway for the replenishment from folic acid of the eNOS co-factor, tetrahydrobiopterin.

α TOCOPHEROL AND PREVENTION OF ISCHAEMIC HEART DISEASE

According to the lipid oxidation hypothesis, LDL needs to be oxidised in order to enter the macrophage via a scavenger receptor.[1,2] The putative key role of LDL oxidation engendered the possibility that anti-oxidants would have therapeutic benefit in prevention of atheroma by inhibiting the LDL oxidation and thus its uptake into macrophages. Several strands of circumstantial evidence support the idea that anti-oxidants are beneficial.

Circumstantial evidence of benefit from vitamin E

The first is the inverse correlation between median levels of α-tocopherol measured in plasma and the incidence of ischaemic heart disease in several different countries.[3] The negative slope of the line relating incidence and α-tocopherol concentration (measured as a fraction of the total cholesterol in which it is dissolved *in vivo*) is of similar steepness to the positive slope relating total cholesterol, or LDL, to risk of myocardial infarction in the 7 Countries studies. In addition, there appear to be fewer outliers in the vitamin E data, which has been used as one possible explanation of the 'French Paradox': why the French have less than half the risk of ischaemic heart disease of the average

British patient, with a median serum LDL value that is only slightly lower than the British figure.

The second piece of circumstantial data is the lower concentrations of vitamin E found in the blood of patients with ischaemic heart disease compared to controls.[4] This finding is independent of differences between the groups in other risk factors that themselves are likely to alter vitamin E intake, especially smoking and the intake of saturated fat rich diets.

The third strand is the large case-control or cohort studies of patients who purchase vitamin E supplements. The largest of these, in women health professionals in the USA, found an approximately 40% reduction but only in women purchasing at least 100-200 mg/day.[5] A more recent study appeared to contradict this result in reporting a 7 year follow-up of postmenopausal women in whom dietary but not supplementary vitamin E caused a similar reduction to the Boston study.[5,6] However, the latter could not control for duration of vitamin E or of initiation of supplementary treatment after the initial questionnaire, and these discrepancies merely highlight probably the difficulties in drawing definite conclusions from non-randomised observational studies.

Effect of vitamin E on *ex vivo* oxidation of LDL

Fourthly, LDL can be oxidised *ex vivo* by incubating it in the presence of oxidising agents like cupric ions, haem, or hydrogen peroxide. The efficacy of anti-oxidants, and a comparison of doses, can then be performed by measuring the lag time to production of oxidation products — usually measured as thiobarbituric acid reacting substances (TBARS).

In a single centre, double-blind, parallel placebo-controlled trial, healthy volunteers (total n = 42) were randomised to receive placebo, 500, 1 000 or 1 500 IU/day of vitamin E (D-alpha-tocopherol) for a period of six weeks. Lag time to LDL oxidation was significantly prolonged and oxidation rate significantly slowed at all dose levels of vitamin E, indicating a threshold effect from 500 IU/day. Compared to placebo, there were dose-related prolongations up to 35% on 1 500 IU/day, and slowing in oxidation rate up to 25%. Changes in plasma vitamin E concentration correlated with the change in lag time (r = 0.61, p < 0.001) and oxidation rate (r = 0.55, p < 0.001).[7]

Presence of oxidised LDL in human atheroma

Lipids and oxidised lipids were analysed by GC and GC-MS in necropsy samples of human atheroma and normal aorta. The latter were detected in amounts proportional to cholesterol in all the atheroma samples but not in normal aorta.[8]

Protection by anti-oxidants against LDL cyto-toxicity of endothelial cells

Heme can rapidly generate oxidized LDL, which then becomes cytotoxic to cultured vascular endothelial cells. 10

human volunteers were given 800 IU daily of DL-alpha-tocopherol acetate alone or in combination with 1 000 mg of ascorbic acid for 2 weeks. LDL resistance to heme oxidation *ex vivo*, as measured by the lag time for conjugated-diene formation, increased by as much as threefold while LDL α tocopherol increased from 11 ±2 to 26 ±6 molecules per LDL particle (P <.001). Cytotoxicity to porcine aortic endothelial cells incubated with LDL conditioned with heme plus H_2O_2 or with copper was completely prevented. These measurements reverted to their presupplement levels within 2 weeks after participants stopped taking antioxidant supplements and were reproduced in 4 subjects taking 800 IU of DL- α tocopherol acetate supplements alone but not in the same subjects taking 1 000 mg ascorbic acid supplements alone.[9]

PROSPECTIVE DATA

The fairly impressive dossier of circumstantial data does not of course come close to proving either the lipid oxidation hypothesis or the value of α tocopherol, and it was the former of these aims which was addressed by our first Cambridge Heart Anti-Oxidant Study (CHAOS-1).[10] 2 002 patients with angiographically proven coronary artery disease were randomised to receive blinded α tocopherol or placebo for approximately $1\frac{1}{2}$ years, in addition to other medication prescribed by their doctors. 6 months after the last patient was recruited into the trial, a census was performed of all the myocardial infarctions and deaths which had occurred. Follow-up of 98% of the patients was achieved, providing details of 55 non-fatal myocardial infarctions and 62 deaths (of which 50 were cardiovascular). Of these endpoints, there was a highly significant reduction in the myocardial infarctions from 41 in the placebo group to 14 in the α tocopherol group. There was a slight and non-significant excess of deaths from all causes in the α tocopherol group. Because of the study design, this trial did not have sufficient power to permit conclusions about the reason for the disparity in treatment effects on cardiovascular deaths and non-fatal myocardial infarctions. The discrepancy may be due to chance alone or it may reflect a difference in anti-oxidant effect on the biological processes leading to death and those leading to non-fatal myocardial infarction. Most of the deaths occurred in the early part of the follow up period, perhaps before any putative beneficial effect on atheromatous plaques could have occurred. It seems likely that the process of angiography will enhance risk of plaque rupture in patients with unstable lesions, and unlikely that this is affected by α tocopherol. Indeed, our recent analysis of outcome on randomised treatment (as against the previously published intention-to-treat analysis) showed that most ischaemic deaths occurred in patients not taking α tocopherol. In addition, the deaths certified (most without necropsy evidence) as due to ischaemic heart disease will include deaths due to causes less likely to be responsive to alpha tocopherol treatment (for example,

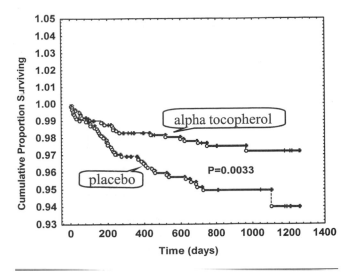

Figure 4-1. Intention-to-treat analysis of non-fatal myocardial infarction in patients randomised to α-tocopherol or placebo during CHAOS.

arrhythmias, progression of heart failure or peri-operative complications). We have also recently completed an analysis of deaths reported to the National Statistical Register by the time randomised treatment ended in March 1996, 9 months after the final trial census. The 116 deaths by then outnumbered reported myocardial infarction, and in a Cox regression analysis NYHA at baseline was seen to be much the most important predictor of outcome (Figs 4-1, 4-2). It seems likely that in a CHAOS type of population, risk of myocardial infarction falls after surgical correction, and follow-up should not be prolonged when conducting such studies. Whether there is a true adverse effect on early mortality cannot be ascertained from these data and must await the results of longer term multicentre trials designed with mortality as a primary endpoint. A recent study of warfarin and aspirin, in a similar patient group, has also found a discrepancy between non-fatal and fatal events, as has several primary prevention trials.[11,12] Indeed, few treatments including aspirin have been shown to reduce mortality in patients with angina.

GENETIC VARIATION IN eNOS IN CHAOS

Among explanations which we and others have advanced for the much greater influence of LDL-lowering and, probably, oxidised-LDL lowering treatments on cardiac events than on coronary artery calibre is improved endothelial function.[13] We therefore postulated that α tocopherol was protecting nitric oxide (NO) from inactivation, and that in some ischaemic heart disease patients the defect in NO production is primary rather than secondary to the disease. Mutation scanning of the eNOS (NOS3) gene revealed several polymorphisms of which the only one affecting amino acid coding was a glutamate to aspartate substitution at

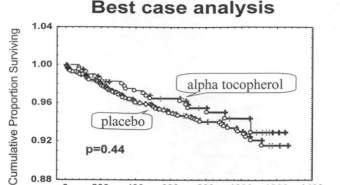

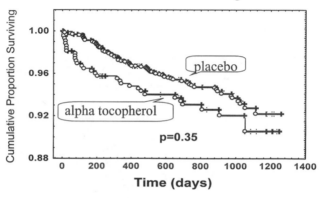

*Figure 4-2. On randomised treatment analysis of deaths in CHAOS.
The graphs are the Kaplan-Meier curve of survival in compliant patients
only, up to the end of randomised treatment in March 1996. The best case
graph assumes that compliant patients were those who were documented
as taking all their drugs up to the end of the trial, or to their primary
event. The worst case graph assumes that in addition, patients who died
during the first 3 months of treatment, before follow-up drug could be re-
quested, were compliant.*

codon 298.[14] Although such substitutions can cause marked
functional loss,[15] the glutamate at this site is present only in
the endothelial isoform, and is not obviously essential for
function.[16] Nevertheless, a preliminary study comparing
frequency of the asp298 variant in 298 CHAOS patients
with 130 healthy controls showed an odds ratio of 7.1 for
the homozygotes, allowing for differences in other risk factors between the groups.[14] Because the CHAOS patients
were not in so-called Hardy-Weinberg equilibrium, and
specifically there was a deficit of heterozygotes, the result
needs confirmation; however, it has been suggested that not
all effects of eNOS activation may be beneficial when there
is limited tetrahydrobiopterin (co-factor) available,[17] and
the heterozygote advantage (if reproduced) would be nice
confirmation of this idea.

Homocysteine, Folate and Heart Disease

An elevated homocysteine level has been known for 30 years to cause premature vascular disease when homozygous mutations in the vitamin B6 dependent cystathionine β synthase or methylene tetrahydrofolate reductase (mthfr) cause the rare monogenic syndrome of homocysteinuria. In the last few years, however, it has become clear that there is also a quantitative relationship between elevated homocysteine and risk of ischaemic heart disease which makes homocysteine as major a risk factor as cholesterol. Thus in a meta-analysis of all studies published up to 1995, Boushey et al calculated an odds ratio for ischaemic heart disease of a 5 μmol/L homocysteine increment at 1.6 for men and 1.8 for women.[18] This concentration of homocysteine represents about a 50% increase above average. A total of 10% of the population's coronary heart disease risk appeared attributable to homocysteine. Unlike cholesterol, what is particularly exciting about the recognition of homocysteine as a risk factor is the likelihood that this risk can be reversed by simple vitamin treatment. Homocysteine can be metabolised by methylation or sulfuration, the latter by the B6 dependent enzyme mentioned above, the former by a vitamin B12 dependent enzyme, methionine synthase, which is effectively also folate dependent as the substrate is methyltetrahydrofolate. In various studies, all three vitamins have achieved substantial reductions in plasma homocysteine levels. Folic acid has received the most attention, and a recent review of all studies suggests that in patients with hyperhomocysteinaemia, folic acid is as effective treatment as are statins in the reduction of hypercholesteraemia.[19] The response varies with basal levels of B6, B12 and, above all, folate, suggesting that homocysteine is regulated by variations in each of these vitamins within the physiological range. The response to B12 and folic acid is slightly additive, achieving maximum falls in the range 40-50%. B6 is most effective in reducing the peaks seen after methionine loading, when homocysteine can be metabolised only via the sulfuration pathway. The effect of folic acid appears to be dose related up to about 600 μg daily, which exceeds normal dietary intake even with the advent of cereal and flour fortification in some countries.[20] However, much higher doses, up to 10 mg, have been studied and may be required to achieve rapid loading of tissue stores in patients at high risk.

To date, the only prospective data available is for folic acid and B6, from the 80082 healthy women in the Nurses' Health Study whose intake of folate and vitamin B6 was derived from a detailed food frequency questionnaire. During 14 years of follow-up, there were 658 cases of nonfatal myocardial infarction and 281 cases of fatal CHD. After controlling for other cardiovascular risk factors, the relative risks of CHD between extreme quintiles were 0.69 for folate (median intake, 696 *vs.* 158 μg/day) and 0.67 for vitamin B6 (median intake, 4.6 *vs* 1.1 mg/day). Controlling for the same variables, the RR was 0.55 (95% CI, 0.41-0.74) among women in the highest quintile of both folate and vitamin B6 intake compared with the opposite extreme.[21] It is not certain that the assumed benefit of the vitamins is from reduction in homocysteine; in several other studies, the inverse relationship between vitamin levels and risk are partly or wholly independent of homocysteine levels, especially for B6, and B12 (which is more effective than B6 in lowering homocysteine) does not on its own appear protective in epidemiological studies.[22]

One speculative alternative mechanism by which folic acid may be beneficial is by protection of the essential co-factor for eNOS, tetrahydrobiopterin. Methyltetrahydrofolate has been shown to reverse endothelial dysfunction *in vivo* in hypercholesterolaemia, and *in vitro* to prevent free oxygen radical formation by eNOS.[23] We have been interested in a little known reaction described by Kaufman by which methyltetrahydrofolate can shuttle back to methylene tetrahydrofolate and at the same time re-activate inactive quininoid dihydrobiopterin to tetrahydrobiopterin.[24] This reaction is probably unimportant most of the time but could become important under conditions of low tetrahydrobiopterin concentrations as seem to be present in atheromatous vessels or vessels of smokers.[25,26] Kaufman suggested that the reaction may occur only under low B12 concentrations when its methyl groups otherwise become trapped in methyltetrahydrofolate; in this case the suggested benefit of folate supplementation may be negated by concurrent B12 supplementation.

These speculations will be answered in the next few years by outcome trials of various vitamin B doses and cocktails. Our own CHAOS-TWO (Cambridge Heart Anti-Oxidant Study — Trial With Other vitamins) started in 1997 as a simple comparison of folic acid 5 mg daily with placebo, in 4000 patients with proven ischaemic heart disease. Approximately half the patients are recruited with stable angina and positive coronary angiograms, while half are recruited during unstable episodes of angina or myocardial infarction. The outcomes are as in CHAOS-1. Other trials, such as the Oxford based SEARCH, are using a combination of folic acid and B12. Because of the possible extra effects of folic acid, and the value of extrapolating from any benefit to the promotion of fresh fruit and vegetables, it will be of interest eventually to compare the trials with single and combination vitamins.

GENETICS OF HYPERHOMOCYSTEINAEMIA

The existence of two separate pathways governing homocysteine levels, and more than one enzyme within these, makes homocysteine an excellent target for research into candidate genes for ischaemic heart disease (Fig 4-3). The genes for methionine synthase (the B12 dependent enzyme which methylates homocysteine) and cystathionine β synthase have common polymorphisms, whilst the previous step in the methylation pathway, mthfr, has a thermolabile variant due to an alanine to valine substitution.[27,28] A num-

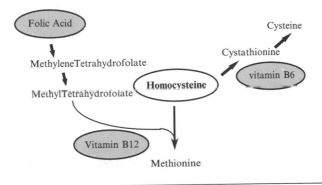

Figure 4-3. Schema of homocysteine metabolism.
The schema illustrates how 3 vitamins play an essential role in the control of homocysteine levels.

ber of studies have found significantly higher homocysteine levels in patients homozygous for the variant, mainly in patients with low folate levels, but there is less agreement on whether the variant is commoner in ischaemic heart disease.[29] Our own studies, in which we have used the same 298 CHAOS and 130 control samples as for the eNOS mutation, show that the variant in mthfr is the only one of the three genes just discussed to be associated with plasma homocysteine or ischaemic heart disease.[30] A meta-analysis of published studies suggests the interesting possibility that the mutation is associated with stable angina but not myocardial infarction. Since we also have preliminary evidence that our eNOS mutation is commoner in ischaemic heart disease than myocardial infarction patients, the importance of defining the patients in such studies cannot be over-emphasized. Our expectation is that several more mutations exist, of which some like that in mthfr may increase requirement for folate, B12 or B6.[31]

CONCLUSION

Foods rich in vitamin E (oily fruit and vegetables) or folic acid (most fruit and vegetables, especially greens and potatoes) may now be assumed to protect against ischaemic heart disease. Prospective trials of these are beginning to show that the epidemiological data in support of vitamin supplementation may also be correct, with the interesting additional expectation that the advent of genetic profiling will permit early identification of subjects requiring such supplements.

REFERENCES

1. Steinberg D. Antioxidant vitamins and coronary heart disease. *N Engl J Med* 1993; 328: 1487–1489.

2. Mitchinson MJ. Macrophages, oxidised lipids and atherosclerosis. *Med Hypotheses* 1983; 12: 171–178.

3. Gey KF. Inverse correlation of vitamin E and ischemic heart disease. *Int J Vitam Nutr Res Suppl* 1989; 1989; 30:224–31:–31.

4. Riemersma RA, Wood DA, Macintyre CC, Elton RA, Gey KF, Oliver MF. Risk of angina pectoris and plasma concentrations of vitamin A, C, and E and carotene. *Lancet* 1991; 337:1–5.

5. Stampfer MJ, Hennekens CH, Manson JE, Colditz GA, Rosner B, Willett WC. Vitamin E consumption and the risk of coronary disease in women. *N Engl J Med* 1993; 328:1444–1449.

6. Kushi LH, Folsom AR, Prineas RJ, Mink PJ, Wu Y, Bostick RM. Dietary antioxidant vitamins and death from coronary heart disease in postmenopausal women. *N Engl J Med* 1996; 334:1156–1162.

7. Simons LA, Von Konigsmark M, Balasubramaniam S. What dose of vitamin E is required to reduce susceptibility of LDL to oxidation? *Aust N Z J Med* 1996; 26: 496–503.

8. Carpenter KL, Taylor SE, Ballantine JA, Fussell B, Halliwell B, Mitchinson MJ. Lipids and oxidised lipids in human atheroma and normal aorta. *Biochim Biophys Acta* 1993; 1167:121–130.

9. Keith SJ. Pharmacologic advances in the treatment of schizophrenia. *N Engl J Med* 1997; 337: 851–853.

10. Stephens NG, Parsons A, Schofield PM, et al. Randomised controlled trial of vitamin E in patients with coronary disease:Cambridge Heart Antioxidant Study (CHAOS). *Lancet* 1996; 347:781–786.

11. The MRC General Practice Research Framework. Thrombosis prevention trial:randomised trial of low-intensity oral anticoagulation with warfarin and low-dose aspirin in the primary prevention of ischaemic heart disease in men at increased risk. *Lancet* 1998; 351:233–241.

12. Shepherd J, Cobbe SM, Ford I, et al. Prevention of coronary heart disease with pravastatin in men with hypercholesterolemia. *N Engl J Med* 1995; 333:1301–1307.

13. Anderson TJ, Meredith IT, Yeung AC, Frei B, Selwyn AP, Ganz P. The effect of cholesterol-lowering and antioxidant therapy on endothelium-dependent coronary vasomotion. *N Engl J Med* 1995; 332:488–493.

14. Hingorani AD, Liang CF, Fatibene J, et al. A variant of the endothelial nitric oxide synthase gene is a risk factor for coronary atherosclerosis. *Clin Sci* 1997; 93:18p

15. Koster JC, Blanco G, Mills PB, Mercer RW. Substitutions of glutamate 781 in the Na, K-ATPase alpha subunit demonstrate reduced cation selectivity and an increased affinity for ATP. *J Biol Chem* 1996; 271:2413–2421.

16. Crane BR, Arvai AS, Gachhui R, et al. The structure of nitric oxide synthase oxygenase domain and inhibitor complexes. *Science* 1997; 278:425–431.

17. Wever RM, Luscher TF, Cosentino F, Rabelink TJ. Atherosclerosis and the two faces of endothelial nitric oxide synthase. *Circulation* 1998; 97:108–112.

18. Boushey CJ, Beresford SA, Omenn GS, Motulsky AG. A quantitative assessment of plasma homocysteine as a risk factor for vascular disease. Probable benefits of increasing folic acid intakes. *JAMA* 1995; 274:1049–1057.

19. Homocysteine Lowering Trialists Collaboration. Lowering blood homocysteine with folic acid based supplements:meta-analysis of randomised trials. *BMJ* 1998; 316:894–898.

20. Malinow MR, Duell PB, Hess DL, et al. Reduction of plasma homocysteine leveles by breakfast cereal fortified with folic acid in

patients with coronary heart disease. *N Engl J Med* 1998; 338:1009–1015.

21. Rimm EB, Willett WC, Hu FB, et al. Folate and vitamin B6 from diet and supplements in relation to risk of coronary heart disease among women. *JAMA* 1998; 279:359–364.

22. Graham IM, Daly LE, Refsum HM, et al. Plasma homocysteine as a risk factor for vascular disease. The European Concerted Action Project. *JAMA* 1997; 277:1775–1781.

23. Verhaar MC, Wever RM, Kastelein JJ, van Dam T, Koomans HA, Rabelink TJ. 5-methyltetrahydrofolate, the active form of folic acid, restores endothelial function in familial hypercholesterolemia. *Circulation* 1998; 97:237–241.

24. Kaufman S. Some metabolic relationships between biopterin and folate:implications for the "methyl trap hypothesis". *Neurochem Res* 1991; 16:1031–1036.

25. Stampfer MJ, Rimm EB. Folate and cardiovascular disease. Why we need a trial now (editorial; comment). *JAMA* 1996; 275:1929–1930.

26. Higman DJ, Strachan AM, Buttery L, et al. Smoking impairs the activity of endothelial nitric oxide synthase in saphenous vein. *Arterioscler Thromb Vasc Biol* 1996; 16:546–552.

27. Frosst P, Blom HJ, Milos R, et al. A candidate genetic risk factor for vascular disease:a common mutation in methylenetetrahydrofolate reductase (letter). *Nat Genet* 1995; 10:111–113.

28. Leclerc D, Campeau E, Goyette P, et al. Human methionine synthase:cDNA cloning and identification of mutations in patients of the cblG complementation group of folate / cobalamin disorders. *Hum Mol Genet* 1996; 5:1867–1874.

29. Ma J, Stampfer MJ, Hennekens CH, et al. Methylenetetrahydrofolate reductase polymorphism, plasma folate, homocysteine, and risk of myocardial infarction in US physicians. *Circulation* 1996; 94:2410–2416.

30. Hockly E, Ashby MJ, Brown MJ. Influence of mutations in methylene tetrahydrofolate reductase, methionine synthase and cystathionine synthase on plasma homocysteine and risk of ischaemic heart disease. *Clin Sci* 1998; 94:1p–21p. (Abstract)

31. Guttormsen AB, Ueland PM, Nesthus I, et al. Determinants and vitamin responsiveness of intermediate hyperhomocysteinemia. The Horldaland homocysteine study. *J Clin Invest* 1996; 98:2174–2183.

CHAPTER 5

Molecular Cardiology into the New Millennium

Hugh Watkins

INTRODUCTION

This text describes a personal view about which aspects of the "molecular revolution" are set to have the most impact on cardiovascular research and practice in the near future. The field of molecular cardiology is, of course, potentially very broad. This review will focus on the applications of molecular *genetics* in particular, reflecting the view that this is the field that offers most in terms of new understanding of the diseases that are important in cardiovascular medicine.

Evolution of approaches to cardiovascular pathophysiology

In order to look forward it is useful to consider first the existing impact of molecular and cellular biology in cardiovascular medicine. Classically, the heart has been viewed very simply as a pump with electrical and mechanical/hydraulic aspects and the vasculature as merely a conduit. It is perhaps because this simple morphological approach has worked reasonably well that cardiology has been slow to embrace the more fundamental scientific approaches of molecular and cellular biology. The 1980s and 1990s saw a description of processes at the molecular and cellular level, providing much more detailed observations of the pathophysiology of various cardiac disorders.

But despite this, many disorders remain very crudely characterised or defined, such that often it is unknown whether the accompanying molecular abnormalities are primary or secondary phenomena. A typical example here would be the changes seen in myocardial hypertrophy and the decompensation into heart failure, where multiple abnormalities are described but which tend to vary from model to model and are of unknown significance. The 1990s has seen the molecular genetic dissection of a number of important inherited cardiac diseases which illustrate how molecular tools can define the actual origins of disease. In the new millennium we will see the use of molecular genetic approaches to better understand the common degenerative cardiovascular diseases and to provide new routes to intervention.

Molecular genetics

While "molecular biology" describes the central dogma that DNA is transcribed into RNA which is translated into protein and thereby drives all biological processes, "molecular genetics" describes specifically the study of inheritance at the molecular level. The study of molecular genetics is extremely powerful as the rules of inheritance will allow disease gene identification as well as genetic manipulation. The new biology will therefore drive an evolution of approaches to therapy (Savill, 1997).

Evolution of approaches to therapy

Classical description of cardiovascular physiology led to assays for conventional pharmacological approaches for drug discovery. The vast majority of cardiovascular agents have been discovered by systematic screening of compounds in such assays. With the molecular and cellular description that developed in the 1980s came structural biology and thereafter, for the first time, rational drug design. For example, knowledge of carboxypeptidase structure led to the design of potential inhibitors of the angiotensin-converting enzyme, which ultimately yielded captopril (Ondetti et al, 1977). Similarly, the ability to clone, manipulate and express protein products through genetic engineering yielded tPA and later derivatives (Pennica et al, 1983). The power to generate monoclonal antibodies has also had a major impact on cardiology, for example antibodies to the platelet IIb/IIIa receptor (Hanson et al, 1988). Molecular genetic approaches will be used next, both to identify novel targets and to facilitate patient selection for more specific use of pharmaceutical agents. No doubt, some approaches to therapy based on discoveries of new targets will depend upon gene therapy.

GENETIC CONTRIBUTION TO DISEASE

The genetic contribution to disease occurs across a spectrum, ranging from conditions which are entirely genetic in their make-up to those in which risk determinants are entirely environmental (Figure 5-1). Monogenic disorders are inherited conditions where a single specific mutation is sufficient to cause the disease. Depending upon the protein product and its mechanism of action, mutations in such disease genes can have either a dominant or recessive effect, and depending upon the localisation of the gene in genome can be either autosomal, ex-linked or transmitted maternally with the mitochondrial genome. Examples of cardiovascular single gene disorders which have been elucidated

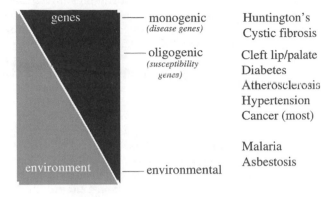

genes	— monogenic *(disease genes)*	Huntington's Cystic fibrosis
	— oligogenic *(susceptibility genes)*	Cleft lip/palate Diabetes Atherosclerosis Hypertension Cancer (most)
environment	— environmental	Malaria Asbestosis

Figure 5-1 The relative contributions of genetic and environmental factors in disease pathogenesis

in recent years include hypertrophic cardiomyopathy (Watkins et al, 1995b) and the long QT syndrome (Keating 1995). It is apparent, however, that the clinically important cardiovascular diseases are those for which there is clear evidence of genetic susceptibility but where variants of the susceptibility genes are neither necessary nor sufficient to cause the disease. Instead, these diseases (such as coronary artery disease and hypertension) represent the impact of a number of susceptibility variants which each alter the threshold above which the disease is manifest. These complex traits, which are just becoming genetically tractable, will be the important target of molecular cardiology in the new millennium.

Genetic mapping

Genes can be mapped by purely positional techniques that allow their identification without necessitating assumptions about their function. Genes which are on different chromosomes are inherited independent of one another within families. Genes which are on the same chromosome will tend to be co-inherited some of the time depending upon their distance apart and therefore the likelihood of recombination during meioses. With the genome project has come an explosion in the availability of DNA markers scattered throughout the human chromosomes that can be used to look for regions which show co-inheritance with disease genes. These markers are now sufficiently densely mapped to allow mapping not just of disease genes but also of susceptibility genes in complex traits. From now on, more limiting than genetic markers will be the availability of the appropriate clinical genetic material, i.e. affected individuals or families.

Mapping single-gene disorders

Large autosomal dominant pedigrees with monogenic disorders such as hypertrophic cardiomyopathy can be mapped by systematically searching each chromosome for a marker that is co-inherited with disease, and will provide sufficient genetic power to identify a sub-region of a chromosome involved. Such a region, for example containing 10 cM of DNA (about 10 million base pairs) may contain dozens of human genes. Nevertheless, fragments of a large proportion of these have been mapped and increasingly it is possible to identify the complement of genes in a particular region that could be candidates for the disease because of their position and putative biological role. Mapping of single gene disorders is therefore accelerating with the successful use of the candidate gene approach, less often is it necessary to positionally clone large tracts of novel DNA. This combined "positional candidate" approach has led to the identification of an array of cardiovascular disease genes (see Table 5-1). This reductionist approach has proved a very powerful tool in furthering our biological understanding of the heart and circulation. Previously idiopathic conditions are now understood at the molecular level. For example familial hypertrophic cardiomyopathy is known to be a disease of the cardiac sarcomere, i.e. the contractile proteins that generate the force of contraction (Thierfelder et al, 1994). This condition also illustrates the common finding of genetic heterogeneity, whereby an apparently single clinical disorder actually reflects a group of genetically distinct, but related, disorders (Watkins et al, 1995a).

Cardiomyopathies:	
HCM	contractile proteins (x 7)
X linked dilated	Dystrophin
Mitochondrial myopathies	tRNAs

Arrhythmias:	
LQT	cardiac K^+ & Na^+ channels
Jervell Lange-Nielsen	recessive, KVLQT1 & minK

Vascular disorders:	
Marfan syndrome	Fibrillin
Supravavular aortic stenosis	Elastin
HHT	Endoglin
Familial hypercholesterolaemia	LDL receptor
Hypobetalipoproteinaemia	Apo B
Homocystinuria	Cystathione synthase

Congenital heart disease:	
Holt Oram syndrome	TBX5

Table 5-1 Cardiovascular single-gene disorders elucidated at a molecular level

Application of genetic advances in single gene disorders

In a monogenic trait where there is an approximate one to one relationship between the mutation of the disease, clinical application is theoretically straightforward. Experience shows, however, that even apparent single gene disorders actually are significantly affected by an individuals genetic background and by the environment. Experience in handling this relatively simple genetic information will be very important for developing the expertise for using more complex susceptibility information. Genetic diagnosis based on the presence of a specific mutation opens the way to preclinical diagnosis which can be important in disorders associated with childhood mortality. Genetic classification, based on a diversity of mutations within the disease gene or a diversity of disease genes, provides a new tool for better categorising a disease. Experiences in single gene disorders again illustrate the power of this approach. Different mutations within the myosin heavy chain gene that cause hypertrophic cardiomyopathy are associated with widely different prognosis but similar extents of hypertrophy (Watkins et al, 1992). Different disease genes in hypertrophic cardiomyopathy are associated with different patterns of penetrance and different prognosis (Watkins et al, 1992; Moolman et al, 1997). Notably, the demonstration of mutations in myosin binding protein-C have indicated a late onset form of hypertrophic cardiomyopathy that has not been recognised previously as affected individuals will not have been seen to have familial disease (Niimura et al, 1998). An important goal of a genetic classification will be disease-gene guided treatment. An exciting illustration of this concept comes from the genetic heterogeneity in the long QT syndrome where individuals with a mutation affecting the sodium channel gene SCN5A respond to sodium channel blocking agents such as mexilitine, while patients with mutations in the potassium channel gene HERG respond to potassium supplementation (Schwartz et al, 1995; Priori et al, 1996; Compton et al, 1996).

GENETIC ANALYSIS IN COMPLEX TRAITS

The list of cardiovascular single-gene disorders that have been elucidated is growing fast, but this rate of progress will slow as most of the important disorders are already in hand. Equally, while our understanding of these disorders is biologically very important, together they are not numerically important cardiac diseases. Importantly, classical genetic epidemiological analyses also indicate a major genetic component in the aetiology of diseases such as hypertension and coronary artery disease and cardiovascular "risk factors" such as diabetes, insulin-resistance and left ventricular hypertrophy. In these quantitative traits, similarities in phenotype between first degree relatives are not dichotomous but rather are spread throughout the range, indicating the cumulative effect of multiple genes.

Thus, in studies of blood pressure, there is a graded relationship between blood pressure in probands (whether hypertensive or not) and recordings in their first degree relatives which implies that variation in the genes that cause hypertension is also responsible for variations in blood pressure across the range.

Nature vs. Nurture: measurement of the genetic effect

Much has been learned about the genetic component of these diseases through twin studies, for example comparisons between monozygotic and dizygotic twins (who share 100% and 50% of their genes respectively) and between monozygotic twins reared together as opposed to those reared apart (to discern environmental influences). An important parameter in quantitative traits is the Relative Risk Ratio (λ), for example the relative risk of siblings of an affected individual over and above the population risk is λs. For hypertrophic cardiomyopathy where siblings carry a 1:2 risk and where the population risk is 1:500, $\lambda s = 250$. An example of a strongly genetically influenced complex trait is insulin dependent diabetes with a λs of 15; as such, genetic progress in this disorder has been very promising (Bennett and Todd, 1996). Relative risks in hypertension and coronary artery disease are (depending on the selection of the cases) in the region of $\lambda s = 2-4$. Thus, while it is reasonable to expect that these disorders are now becoming genetically tractable (Julier et al, 1997), efforts will need to be made to enrich for genetic effect in future studies.

Enriching for genetic effect

An important concept is that of the "intermediate phenotype". If a component of a complex disease process can be identified, for example a biochemically measurable risk factor such as lipid abnormalities in coronary disease, then its genetic determinants will be simpler and more accessible than the overall phenotype (Assmann, 1990; Dammerman and Breslow, 1995). Attention to intermediate phenotypes has been critical in the successfully genetic analysis of complex diseases such as asthma (Daniels et al, 1996). Similarly, selection of extreme forms of the disease enrich for the genetic effect and increase the relative risk. Typically individuals with early onset disease, a strong family history, severe disease or an extreme trait will be needed for any genetic study. Twin data in coronary artery disease illustrate the increased genetic effect in relatives of individuals with early myocardial infarction (Marenberg et al, 1994). Individuals who have a first degree relative who died of an MI below the age of 55 for a male, or 65 for a female, have a fourfold increased risk of dying of MI themselves. Thus a strong family history such as this is a comparable risk factor to lifelong smoking. In contrast, the relative risk conferred by a first degree relative (e.g. a parent) dying of a myocardial infarction around the age of 70 is only in the order of 1.5 (Table 5-2).

| Age at death | Relative Hazard (95% CI) | |
	Men	Women
Monozygotics twins		
36-55	8.1 (2.7-24.5)	} 15.0 (7.1-31.9)
56-65	6.0 (3.3-10.8)	
66-75	3.8 (2.5-6.0)	3.8 (2.2-6.7)
Dizygotic twins		
36-55	3.8 (1.4-10.5)	} 2.6 (1.0-7.1)
56-65	2.5 (1.6-4.0)	
66-75	1.7 (1.3-2.3)	1.8 (1.2-2.8)

Table 5-2 Relative hazards of death from myocardial infarction among twins by age of death of the first twin to die from MI, controlled for risk factors (data from Marenberg et al.).

Approaches to identification of susceptibility genes: association and linkage

Genetic association describes a situation where a specific DNA variant is more prevalent in cases with a given disease than among controls. This may be because the variant is itself responsible for disease susceptibility; alternatively, the variant may be merely a marker which is in linkage disequilibrium with the biologically important variant because the two are sufficiently close to one another to tend to be inherited together on an ancestral founder chromosome. Association that results from the variant in question having a causal effect will be replicable in our related populations; association resulting from linkage disequilibrium may differ from one population to another depending upon founder effects. Because the marker variant and the true susceptibility variant must remain together over many generations for the association to be detectable in unrelated cases, association only identifies variants over very short genetic distances. In practice, this limits tests for association to tests exploring the effect of specific variants in designated candidate genes. Hence, this approach may validate the role of putative candidate genes but is unlikely to disclose totally novel susceptibility genes.

Because association studies are performed in case:control populations (which are freely available from other clinical trial or epidemiological research) these studies are becoming very numerous, particularly in relation to coronary artery disease (Table 5-3) (Cambien et al, 1992; Jeunemaitre et al 1992; Moor et al, 1995; Ye et al, 1996; Schmitz et al, 1996; Norlund et al, 1997; Anderson et al, 1997). It is already apparent that some associations are robust (particularly those between a variant in a gene and a biochemical quantitative trait, e.g. Tiret et al, 1992), whereas others are not reproduced in subsequent studies — especially those relating to a complex phenotype such as myocardial infarction. The situation is analogous to that in the early days of HLA associations, and the reasons for false positive associations are the same. Type I errors are likely when multiple

Positive studies	Negative studies
Apo B	
Apo E	
Apo (a)	
ACE (D/I)	✓
PAI-1 (4G/5G)	✓
MTHFR	✓
Platelet glycoprotein IIIa	✓
Paraoxonase	✓
tPA	✓
Factor VII	✓
Thrombomodulin	

Table 5-3 Examples of association studies with variants in candidate genes for coronary artery disease. Variants in lipoprotein genes are consistently associated with plasma lipid levels and tend to associate with CAD risk in studies of sufficient power. The variants in the more "novel" candidate genes have been found to associate with CAD risk in some studies, but significant associations have later been excluded in other studies. See text for references.

investigators perform unrelated and under-powered studies on small populations; inevitably some of these studies will produce apparently statistically significant results which will lead to publication bias (Samani et al, 1996). Subsequent, epidemiologically sized, studies are tending to exclude significant associations (see Table 5-3) (Lindpaintner et al, 1995; Ridker et al, 1997a & b). Sub-group analysis can exacerbate this problem (particularly when it is performed post hoc) unless proper correction is made for the number of hypotheses tested. The original observation of an association between the D allele of the ACE gene with myocardial infarction was performed in a reasonably large study (Cambien et al, 1992) but the significance of the association depended in large part on the strong association in a "low risk" sub-group of males. Subsequent studies have not confirmed a major association and have excluded a particular association in this low risk group.

In addition to the above concerns, which are equally relevant to all epidemiological studies, genetic association studies are additionally vulnerable to genetic admixture. If cases and controls are not extremely closely matched for ethnicity (i.e. gene pool) an apparently associated allele may simply be more common in the population from which the cases are derived. This problem can be avoided in two ways. Carefully designed epidemiologically based population sampling is much more robust than collection of controls from some other selected source — such as subjects which attend for investigation but subsequently found not to have the disease. Alternatively, a family based study allows use of the transmission disequilibrium test (TDT) which will eliminate the problem (Figure 5-2a). If parents of cases are available for genotyping then the preferential transmission of the disease associated allele can be shown by comparing the frequency of this allele that is transmitted to the affected case as opposed to non-transmission. While it can be hard to find living parents of cases who have late onset diseases, the main reason for failure to use the TDT test is that the study population has to be specifically designed rather than co-opted from other ongoing research. In the future, association studies will become increasingly important because it will become possible to type much denser arrays of variants in known genes. In light of this, large collection of small nuclear families, rather than case:control populations, will be a key goal.

Linkage in complex traits

Genetic linkage exists when a variant at an anonymous marker co-segregates with the disease traits within families. In this instance the variant is not itself biologically involved in the disease, but it is near enough to the susceptibility

a) for TDT test

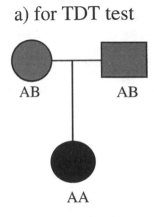

Figure 5-2 *Family structures for use in genetic analysis in complex traits. a) by transmission disequilibrium test (TDT); the excess of a genuine susceptibility allele (A) in cases can be shown to reflect preferential transmission rather than just higher frequency in parents of cases.*

b) for sib-pair analysis

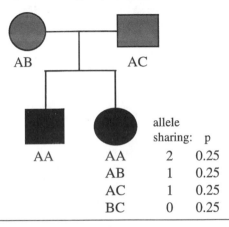

Figure 5-2(b) *allele-sharing methods in affected sib pairs; excess sharing of susceptibility allele (A) in the affected sibs over that predicted by random assortment is in favour of genetic linkage.*

gene to be co-inherited with it within the family. Because co-inheritance is sought within just one or two generations (rather than over many generations from an ancestral founder haplotype) genetic linkage can be detected over much larger genetic distances. Thus markers spaced evenly throughout the genome can be used to systematically search for linkage to susceptibility genes (Weeks and Lathrop, 1995). So long as sufficient genetic power can be achieved to show statistical evidence of linkage to a gene that only contributes to part of the genetic risk, then this is a most powerful technique because it allows identification of complete novel susceptibility genes. In a complex trait it cannot be known whether the susceptibility genes confer dominant or recessive phenotype and this requires a non-model based or non-parametric analysis. In practice this is best achieved by looking for excess allele sharing in pairs of first degree affected relatives. In late onset diseases this usually equates to sibling pairs (see Figure 5-2b). This approach is robust because it does not require knowledge of the genetic model but rather is based on rejecting a model of random segregation, and is potentially powerful because it allows systematic genome screens. Individual nuclear families or sib pairs are not, however, genetically powerful and relatively large populations of stringently ascertained sib pairs are needed in diseases with relatively low relatively risk ratios.

Power estimations in genome screens

The power of an affected sib pair approach depends upon λs (which can be enhanced by selecting extreme forms of the disease) and on the number of genes which contribute to the genetic variance. Thus, in coronary artery disease, available data suggests that one would need to study upwards of 2 000 affected sibling pairs where each sibling has early onset of coronary heart disease to be able to detect genes which individually contribute 10 or 15% of the variants in the phenotype. Despite the demands of this approach it remains potentially very worthwhile. Known genetic contributions to the risk of CHD do not appear to account for all of the genetically transmitted risk; indeed up to 50% of cases with MI do not have obvious risk factors for the disease (Braunwald 1997). This approach therefore has the exciting potential to yield completely new insights into CAD disease pathogenesis (Hamsten, 1996).

CLINICAL TRIALS AND GENETICS

Harnessing trials

From the above it is clear that clinical trial populations or epidemiological study groups are a rich source for both cases and controls for association studies but also to provide index cases for ascertainment of sibling pairs or families for TDT. In addition, prospective epidemiological studies have the advantage that genes which will later cause individuals to die of complications of the disease have not yet been selected out (as they would be in case-control series of survivors). Such studies will be important for the identification of "bad outcome" genes such as those that determine the risk of stroke in hypertension or MI in diabetes.

Because a better understanding of susceptibility genes will allow us to select individuals and match treatments, genetic epidemiology will bring benefit to clinical trials just as much as it will itself benefit from the patient resources.

How will we use Knowledge of Susceptibility Genes ?

Selection of patients; selection of treatments

Given the scale of investment necessary for the identification of susceptibility genes in common cardiovascular diseases such as hypertension and coronary disease it is necessary to consider how the information will be useful. In the first instance, a better understanding of susceptibility genes will allow us to select individuals for treatment and to match them to the most appropriate treatment, in other words to provide for more rational use of existing drugs. Selection can be expected to operate at least at three levels. First, selection by identification of individuals at risk. Existing risk factors are poor predictors of absolute levels of risk for individuals. For example, there may be a graded risk of coronary disease in relation to cholesterol level, or stroke related to blood pressure level, such that reduction in the risk factor reduces risk proportionally. Nevertheless, treatment cannot be offered to everybody because of issues of cost and complications. Identification of "high risk" individuals by taking the most extreme cut-off of the risk factor distribution will indeed correctly target treatment to those individuals but will miss the majority who will go on to develop the disease despite having levels within the "normal range" (see Figure 5-3). Identification of the major sus-

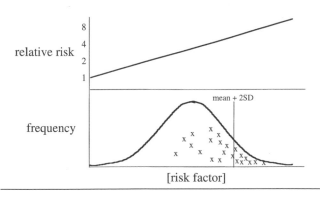

Figure 5-3 *The relationship between a quantitative trait (e.g. total cholesterol or systolic blood pressure) and risk of disease (e.g. CAD or stroke), and the likelihood of affected individuals being in the extremes of the range. A high cut-off (e.g. at 2 SD above the mean) identifies a high risk group but does not identify most cases (illustrated by Xs) who will develop the disease.*

ceptibility genes for given traits will allow the identification of individuals who, for example, have a "normal" cholesterol level but are at significantly elevated risk of MI.

Second, a genetic classification of a disease such as high blood pressure into its constituent parts would be expected to reveal that certain existing treatments are effective in one aetiology but less so in another (Vincent et al, 1997). Thus, the present practice of using the same selection of drugs in all affected individuals may be considerably refined and drugs which are only sometimes effective at present may be very effective within the correct sub-group. Thus analysis of genetic constitution may help direct prescription of existing drugs and may indeed find a niche for drugs which have hitherto not been sufficiently effective for general licensing.

Third, the potential for pharmacogenetic analysis will grow dramatically and should aid identification both of responders, as opposed to non-responders, but also those at risk of adverse effects due to variants in the drug target or metabolism pathway. This is a well established concept which to date has had little impact into general medical practice but will be of growing importance as it becomes easier to first identify important polymorphisms and then to type them routinely (Marshall, 1997).

Novel targets for novel therapies

Although patient selection may be an important issue, the main goal of genome-wide screens for susceptibility genes is identification of novel pathways involved in the disease process. Systematic genome-wide approaches may lead eventually to the identification genetic variants in proteins not previously known to be involved in the disease pathogenesis. The pathogenic role of such variants will have to be established by a variety of "functional genomic" approaches, for example expression studies in vitro or the creation of gene targeted mouse models to recapitulate the phenotype. Biological exploration of the new susceptibility gene product (which may be a completely novel protein or else one already known but not thought to be involved in the disease) will aim to identify a pathway through which the genetic effect is exerted and within which are suitable therapeutic targets. By way of illustration, a genetic analysis of hypertension could have identified the significance of variants in the gene for angiotensinogen even without prior knowledge of the role of the renin-angiotensin system (Jeunemaitre et al, 1992). Subsequent dissection of the pathway would have identified the angiotensin converting enzyme and the angiotensin-II receptor has potential targets amenable to therapeutic manipulation.

Drug therapy or gene therapy?

It might naturally be assumed that because a genetic approach had been taken to identify a novel therapeutic target, that a genetic approach to treatment would be the goal. There is thus much expectation that gene therapy is the intended goal of genetic research. However, in the important cardiovascular disorders which are common (requiring widespread treatment) and chronic (requiring long term treatment) a small molecule drug will be the more important goal. Despite this, a certain investment in gene therapy approaches is to be expected as these may provide earlier routes to treatment, even if limited in their applicability. Thus, if a truly novel protein is identified genetic techniques can be used to block its expression or its action (or if appropriate to replace or enhance its expression) without full knowledge of its structure or biology. For example, the use of antisense or dominant negative alleles may provide the first opportunity to interfere with a novel pathway prior to the development of small molecule drugs.

GENETIC MANIPULATION

Much of the power of molecular genetics relates to the opportunities it provides for genetic manipulation either in man or model organisms. Somatic manipulation that alters the genetic expression of a population of cells, or a given tissue, rather than the genetic constitution of the germline of an individual, includes all the various approaches that come under the title of "gene therapy". Manipulation of the germline (to produce heritable changes) is potentially even more powerful, but of course more complex in the issues it raises. Nevertheless, germline manipulation in model organisms will provide one of the most powerful of biological tools for research.

Cardiovascular gene therapy: Current limitations

A survey of experimental approaches that are currently being tested illustrates the potential, but also the difficulties, of gene therapy approaches. It is fairly easy to devise means of either blocking expression or action of a gene product, of replacing a missing protein or of augmenting expression of a desired protein (see Table 5-4). The main limitations at present relate to the successful targeting of the gene therapy, the proportion of cells that can be transfected and to the duration of expression. It may be relatively easy to devise molecules which will achieve the desired effect, for example an antisense molecule, a ribozyme or a decoy to block a particular process (Gibbons and Dzau, 1996). More difficult has been derivation of vectors for targeting the appropriate cells and promoters for directing controlled expression. For these reasons early trials of gene therapy have involved either ex vivo gene therapy (Grossman et al, 1994) or regional disease processes where local delivery is possible. Hence post-angioplasty re-stenosis or vein graft atherosclerosis are very attractive models because local delivery is both achievable and desirable (Simons et al, 1992; Mann et al, 1997; Channon et al, 1997). Systemic problems such as hypertension or widespread atherosclerosis are less suitable candidates. Similarly, gene therapy will work well where a soluble product from that

Block expression:

antisense
e.g. antisense to c-Myc in restenosis

Block action:

decoy
e.g. E2F decoy to inhibit
proliferation in vein grafts

Replace missing protein:

transient transfection
stable transfection
e.g. NOS adenovirus in vein grafts
e.g. LDL receptor in hepatocytes

Augmented expression:

transient transfection
e.g. VEGF for angiogenesis

Table 5-4 Examples of current approaches to
cardiovascular "gene therapy". See text for references.

proportion of cells that are transfected will have a desired effect on the remaining population of cells, and where temporary expression will achieve a desired effect. Again, efforts to block re-stenosis or early vein graft responses to arterialisation, or to initiate angiogenesis (Baumgartner et al, 1998) are good examples where a transient effect is sufficient. Few systems deliver long term gene expression and the current transfection tends to be associated with immune phenomena either to the vector or to the native protein if previously absent in an individual with an inherited deficiency. There is no doubt that these problems will be, indeed are being, overcome — particularly by developments in vector design. Limitations are dwelt on here primarily to offset undo early expectations and to reiterate that conventional pharmaceutical approaches are likely to remain predominant.

Germline manipulation

Classical transgenic approaches are already one of the mainstays of current cardiovascular research, though their role is likely to grow in the new millennium. The creation of transgenics by pronuclear injection of naked DNA (as opposed to gene targeting, see below) is powerful because it is not constrained unduly by species (Mullins and Mullins, 1996). Transgenic approaches in large animals may ultimately provide a source of non-human organs for transplantation, although this will require a more sophisticated approach to immune modulation and a solution to the justifiable fears regarding zoonoses.

Gene targeting through genetic manipulation in pleuripotent embryonic stem cells which are later re-injected into the developing embryo is a more powerful technique, though with its own limitations. The power stems from the opportunity for ever more refined genetic manipulation: genes may be knocked out or conditionally knocked out (in certain tissues or stages of development), specific mutations may be added or whole chromosomal regions rearranged (Smithies and Maeda, 1996). The chief limitation is that this technology is currently only available in certain mouse strains. While the adaptation of cardiovascular physiology has been very impressive in the mouse (Chien, 1996), this species has inherent differences which will inevitably impact on the way in which certain phenotypes manifest. Gene targeting in larger organisms remains an elusive, but important goal. Steps towards the derivation of embryonic stem cells in other strains and other species (particularly the rat) have been made, and this may have an important impact in coming years (McWhir et al, 1996).

Finally, reports of successful nuclear transfer allowing cloning of a whole organism from a differentiated, adult cell offer exciting, though complex, avenues for future research (Wilmut et al, 1997). While cloning of human individuals will inevitably remain an alarming prospect, derivation of differentiated cell types of genetically (and immunologically) identical composition would offer remarkable possibilities for repair and restoration of disease tissues. The impact of such capabilities might be particularly great in organs such as the heart where cells are otherwise totally differentiated and cell loss, through infarction, underlies one of the commonest causes of human morbidity and mortality.

CONCLUSIONS

The impact of molecular genetic approaches in cardiovascular disease has so far been restricted to the less common inherited forms of heart disease. Nevertheless, the impact has been considerable because of the fundamental biological insights that have been provided in a variety of diseases which were previously of unknown aetiology. The exciting potential for the near future is the application of similar genetic approaches to the important cardiovascular diseases, most of which have a major genetic component. Application of knowledge regarding genetic susceptibility will be complex but will inevitably influence clinical practice in due course. Before this, it is reasonable to hope that totally novel insights into disease pathogenesis are achievable and that these should open the way to novel therapies. The coupling of molecular genetics with clinical epidemiology will be necessary for these genetic discoveries; thereafter, the coupling of molecular genetics with the full range of biological and integrated physiological approaches will be necessary to translate genetic discoveries into clinically useful information.

REFERENCES

Anderson JL, King GJ, Thomson MJ, Todd M, Bair TL, Muhlestein JB, Carlquist JF. A mutation in the methylenetetrahydrofolate reductase gene is not associated with increased risk for coronary artery disease or myocardial infarction. *J Am Coll Cardiol* 1997; 30:1206–1211.

Assmann G. Genes and dyslipoproteinaemias. *Eur Heart J* 1990; 11 Suppl H:4–8.

Baumgartner I, Pieczek A, Manor O, et al. Constitutive expression of phVEGF165 after intramuscular gene tranfer promotes collateral vessel development in patients with critical limb ischemia. *Circulation* 1998; 97:1114–1123.

Bennett ST, Todd JA. Human type 1 diabetes and the insulin gene: principles of mapping polygenes. *Annu Rev Genet* 1996; 30:343–370.

Braunwald E. Shattuck lecture—cardiovascular medicine at the turn of the millennium: triumphs, concerns, and opportunities. *N Engl J Med* 1997; 337:1360–1369.

Bronson SK, Smithies O. Altering mice by homologous recombination using embryonic stem cells. *J Biol Chem* 1994; 269:27155–27158.

Cambien F, Poirier O, Lecerf L, et al. Deletion polymorphism in the gene for angiotensin–converting enzyme is a potent risk factor for myocardial infarction. *Nature* 1992; 359:641–644.

Channon KM, Fulton GJ, Gray JL, et al. Efficient adenoviral gene transfer to early venous bypass grafts: comparison with native vessels. *Cardiovasc Res* 1997; 35:505–513.

Chien KR. Genes and physiology: molecular physiology in genetically engineered animals. *J Clin Invest* 1996; 98:S19–S26.

Compton SJ, Lux RL, Ramsey MR, et al. Genetically defined therapy of inherited long–QT syndrome. Correction of abnormal repolarization by potassium. *Circulation* 1996; 94:1018–1022.

Dammerman M, Breslow JL. Genetic basis of lipoprotein disorders. *Circulation* 1995; 85:505–512.

Daniels SE, Bhattacharrya S, James A, et al. A genome–wide search for quantitative trait loci underlying asthma. *Nature* 1996; 383:247–250.

Gibbons GH, Dzau VJ. Molecular therapies for vascular diseases. *Science* 1996; 272:689–693.

Grossman M, Raper SE, Kozarsky K, et al. Successful ex vivo gene therapy directed to liver in a patient with familial hypercholesterolaemia. *Nat Genet* 1994; 6:335–341.

Hamsten A. Molecular genetics as the route to understanding, prevention, and treatment. *Lancet* 1996; 348:s17–s19.

Hanson SR, Pareti FI, Ruggeri ZM, et al. Effects of monoclonal antibodies against the platelet glycoprotein IIb/IIIa complex on thrombosis and hemostasis in the baboon. *J Clin Invest* 1988; 81:149–158.

Jeunemaitre X, Soubrier F, Kotelevtsev YV, et al. Molecular basis of human hypertension: role of angiotensinogen. *Cell* 1992; 71:169–180.

Julier C, Delepine M, Keavney B, et al. Genetic susceptibility for human familial essential hypertension in a region of homology with blood pressure linkage on rat chromosome 10. *Hum Mol Genet* 1997; 6:2077–2085.

Keating MT. Genetic approaches to cardiovascular disease. Supravalvular aortic stenosis, Williams syndrome, and long–QT syndrome. *Circulation* 1995; 92:142–147.

Keating MT, Sanguinetti MC. Molecular genetic insights into cardiovascular disease. *Science* 1996; 272:681–685.

Lindpaintner K, Pfeffer MA, Kreutz R, et al. A prospective evaluation of an angiotensin–converting–enzyme gene polymorphism and the risk of ischemic heart disease. *N Engl J Med* 1995; 332:706–711.

Mann M, Dzau V. Vein graft gene therapy using E2F decoy oligonucleotides: Target gene inhibition in human veins and long-term resistance to atherosclerosis in rabbits. *Surgical Forum* 48(0): 242 244 1997; 242–244.

Marenberg ME, Risch N, Berkman LF, Floderus B, de Faire U. Genetic susceptibility to death from coronary heart disease in a study of twins. *N Engl J Med* 1994; 330:1041–1046.

Marshall A. Laying the foundations for personalized medicines. *Nat Biotechnol* 1997; 15:954–957.

McWhir J, Schnieke AE, Ansell R, Wallace H, Colman A, Scott AR, Kind AJ. Selective ablation of differentiated cells permits isolation of embryonic stem cell lines from murine embryos with a non-permissive genetic background. *Nat Genet* 1996; 14:223–226.

Moolman JC, Corfield VA, Posen B, Ngumbela K, Seidman C, Brink PA, Watkins H. Sudden death due to troponin T mutations. *J Am Coll Cardiol* 1997; 29:549–555.

Moor E, Silveira A, van't Hooft F, Suontaka AM, Eriksson P, Blomback M, Hamsten A. Coagulation factor VII mass and activity in young men with myocardial infarction at a young age. Role of plasma lipoproteins and factor VII genotype. *Arterioscler Thromb Vasc Biol* 1995; 15:655–664.

Mullins LJ, Mullins JJ. Transgenesis in the rat and larger mammals. *J Clin Invest* 1996; 98:S37–S40.

Niimura H, Bachinski LL, Watkins H, et al. Human cardiac myosin binding protein C mutations cause late-onset familial cardiac hypertrophy. *N Engl J Med* 1998; In Press.

Norlund L, Holm J, Zoller B, Ohlin AK. A common thrombomodulin amino acid dimorphism is associated with myocardial infarction. *Thromb Haemost* 1997; 77:248–251.

Ondetti MA, Rubin B, Cushman DW. Design of specific inhibitors of angiotensin-converting enzyme: new class of orally active antihypertensive agents. *Science* 1977; 196:441–444.

Pennica D, Holmes WE, Kohr WJ, et al. Cloning and expression of human tissue-type plasminogen activator cDNA in E. coli. *Nature* 1983; 301:214–221.

Priori SG, Napolitano C, Cantu F, Brown AM, Schwartz PJ. Differential response to Na+ channel blockade, beta–adrenergic stimulation, and rapid pacing in a cellular model mimicking the SCN5A and HERG defects present in the long-QT syndrome. *Circ Res* 1996; 78:1009–1015.

Ridker PM, Hennekens CH, Lindpaintner K, Stampfer MJ, Miletich JP. Arterial and venous thrombosis is not associated with the 4G/5G polymorphism in the promoter of the plasminogen activator inhibitor gene in a large cohort of US men. *Circulation* 1997; 95:59–62.

Ridker PM, Hennekens CH, Schmitz C, Stampfer MJ, Lindpaintner K. PIA1/A2 polymorphism of platelet glycoprotein IIIa and risks of myocardial infarction, stroke, and venous thrombosis. *Lancet* 1997; 349:385–388.

Samani NJ, Thompson JR, O'Toole L, Channer K, Woods KL. A meta-analysis of the association of the deletion allele of the angiotensin-converting enzyme gene with myocardial infarction. *Circulation* 1996; 94:708–712.

Savill J. Molecular genetic approaches to understanding disease. BMJ 1997; 314:126–129.

Schmitz C, Lindpaintner K, Verhoef P, Gaziano JM, Buring J. Genetic polymorphism of methylenetetrahydrofolate reductase and myocardial infarction. A case-control study. *Circulation* 1996; 94:1812–1814.

Schwartz PJ, Priori SG, Locati EH, et al. Long QT syndrome patients with mutations of the SCN5A and HERG genes have differential responses to Na+ channel blockade and to increases in heart rate. Implications for gene-specific therapy. *Circulation* 1995; 92:3381–3386.

Simons M, Edelman ER, DeKeyser JL, Langer R, Rosenberg RD. Antisense c-myb oligonucleotides inhibit intimal arterial smooth muscle cell accumulation in vivo. *Nature* 1992; 359:67–70.

Smithies O, Maeda N. Gene targeting approaches to complex genetic diseases: atherosclerosis and essential hypertension. *Proc Natl Acad Sci U S A* 1995; 92:5266–5272.

Tiret L, Rigat B, Visvikis S, Breda C, Corvol P, Cambien F, Soubrier F. Evidence, from combined segregation and linkage analysis, that a variant of the angiotensin I-converting enzyme (ACE) gene controls plasma ACE levels. *Am J Hum Genet* 1992; 51:197–205.

Vincent M, Samani NJ, Gauguier D, Thompson JR, Lathrop GM, Sassard J. A pharmacogenetic approach to blood pressure in Lyon hypertensive rats. A chromosome 2 locus influences the response to a calcium antagonist. *J Clin Invest* 1997; 100:2000–2006.

Watkins H, Rosenzweig A, Hwang DS, Levi T, McKenna W, Seidman CE, Seidman JG. Characteristics and prognostic implications of myosin missense mutations in familial hypertrophic cardiomyopathy. *N Engl J Med* 1992; 326:1108–1114.

Watkins H, McKenna WJ, Thierfelder L, et al. Mutations in the genes for cardiac troponin T and alpha-tropomyosin in hypertrophic cardiomyopathy. *N Engl J Med* 1995; 332:1058–1064.

Watkins H, Seidman JG, Seidman CE. Familial hypertrophic cardiomyopathy: a genetic model of cardiac hypertrophy. *Hum Mol Genet* 1995; 4:1721–1727.

Weeks DE, Lathrop GM. Polygenic disease: methods for mapping complex disease traits. *Trends Genet* 1995; 11:513–519.

Wilmut I, Schnieke AE, McWhir J, Kind AJ, Campbell KH. Viable offspring derived from fetal and adult mammalian cells. *Nature* 1997; 385:810–813.

Ye S, Eriksson P, Hamsten A, Kurkinen M, Humphries SE, Henney AM. Progression of coronary atherosclerosis is associated with a common genetic variant of the human stromelysin–1 promoter which results in reduced gene expression. *J Biol Chem* 1996; 271:13055–13060.

CHAPTER 6

Molecular Approaches to Evaluate the Role of Metabolic Genes in Cardiac Hypertrophy and Heart Failure

Michael N. Sack and Daniel P. Kelly

Glossary of molecular biologic terminology used in this chapter:

Cis elements: DNA sequences within an individual gene that are responsible for directing the level of expression of the same gene.

Enhancer: Cis acting elements that can direct a significant increase in transcription independent of their respective position and orientation within a given gene; enhancers can play an important role in the regulation of tissue specific and inducible expression of individual genes.

Gene: The entire DNA sequence necessary for the synthesis of a functional protein (polypeptide) or RNA sequence.

Homology: DNA sequences appear partially identical when genes of different species are compared. It is estimated that the genes of mouse and man are 80% identical, which is considered high level of homology.

Isoforms: Proteins with a similar structure and function. They can be derived from a single gene or physically separate genes.

Knock-out: Gene targeting technique, to delete one allele of a gene through homologous recombination. The exact localization of this deletion is known. Lethality in homologous embryos indicates the essential function of the gene.

Messenger RNA (mRNA): The final RNA molecule formed through precursor RNA splicing and modification of the ends (poly A tail). This is the RNA molecule encompassing all coding sequences and capable of crossing the nuclear membrane to bring the message to the ribosomes for protein synthesis.

Poly A: The polymer of adenine nucleotides that are located at the end of mRNA.

Promoter: The region of a gene that binds RNA polymerase and initiates gene transcription can include DNA elements that regulate various phases of development, target expression of a gene to selective tissues, and confer inducibility in response to defined stimuli. The position of the promoter in relation to the transcription start site is fixed.

Phenotype: Observable characteristics of an organism, resulting from the interaction of its genes and the environment in which development occurs.

Ribosomes: Consist of two unequal subunits bound together by magnesium ions. This cytosolic organelle translates mRNA into its appropriate protein.

Trans acting factor: The regulatory factors not located in the gene itself but direct and regulate the expression of a given gene (e.g., proteins that bind and regulate the promoter region of a gene).

Transcript: Product of transcription (RNA)

Transcription: The synthesis of RNA from a DNA template by the protein RNA polymerase.

Transcription factor: Protein, that can modify transcription levels of a gene through direct binding of specific DNA sequences (cis-elements) of that gene.

Transfection: Introduction of foreign DNA into eukaryotic cells.

Transgenic: A technique used to transfer a gene into the germline of experimental animals that express the exogenous gene. The number of times and the localization of the transgene incorporation into the genome are unpredictable and random.

Translation: The synthesis of proteins from the mRNA template by the ribosomes.

INTRODUCTION

The notion that "energy depletion" as a contributory factor in the transition from compensated cardiac hypertrophy to the decompensated heart failure has been an attractive yet elusive hypothesis to prove. Studying the function of the mitochondria — the main source of oxidative phosphorylation, and thus the "power pack" of the heart, has resulted in conflicting data, indicative of the limitation in the technology used to isolate and measure mitochondrial function. Likewise, studying the high-energy phosphate stores in the failing heart have suggested that the global cardiac stores are modestly reduced or unchanged under basal conditions. However, it has not been possible to date to assess whether there is a limitation in energy generation or in compartmentally available energy stores to maintain cellular function and structure in the transition from cardiac hypertrophy to heart failure (Ingwall, 1993; Katz, 1998; Scheuer, 1993).

To further delineate the role of energy metabolism in the development of cardiac disease, the study of metabolic fuel utilization has been studied extensively. Biochemical and metabolic imaging studies have defined energy fuel utilization in the heart, and demonstrate high levels of regulation during development, in the normal, and, in the diseased heart. During fetal development the heart functions in a relatively hypoxic environment and glucose and lactate are the predominant energy substrates. Postnatally, a switch in energy substrate utilization occurs, so that fatty acids become the predominant substrate used in the adult heart. Studies have shown that myocardial energy substrate utilization reverts to the foetal pattern during cardiac hypertrophy and in the failing heart with decreased fatty acid and increased glucose utilization. In the spontaneously hypertensive rat, Christe and Rodgers (1994) showed an increase in glucose oxidation and a marked suppression of palmitate oxidation in left ventricular hypertrophy compared to the normal ventricle. A recent dual-tracer study in humans demonstrated reduced fatty acid utilization and increased glucose utilization in hearts in a subset of subjects with idiopathic dilated cardiomyopathy (Feinendegen et al, 1995). These results and the results of other published reports are consistent with emerging evidence that a switch in myocardial energy substrate from fatty acids to glucose occurs during the development of cardiac hypertrophy and cardiac failure (Reviewed, Sack et al, 1998). Little is known, however, about the regulatory mechanisms involved in this alteration in cardiac energy metabolism. Moreover, the role of this energy substrate switch as an adaptive versus maladaptive response and its potential contribution to the development of cardiac hypertrophy and the transition to non-ischaemic heart failure are unknown.

MOLECULAR APPROACHES TO STUDY THE FUNCTIONAL ROLE OF ENERGY METABOLISM IN CARDIAC DYSFUNCTION

To address the relative contribution of energy production/ utilization in the development of non-ischaemic cardiac failure scientists have begun studying the molecular basis of energy utilization in the heart. Specifically, delineating the molecular programmes directing energy utilization in the heart, will allow us to dissect out the contribution of energy metabolism to the complex mechanisms responsible for cardiac decompensation. The main approaches can be loosely divided into the study of: molecular genetics; gene regulatory control; genetic engineering (gene targetting) and protein chemistry (structure/function analysis). In this chapter we will discuss studies utilizing these molecular disciplines to evaluate how the field of cardiac metabolism has advanced in the last decade (Figure 6-1). Combining these data, will allow us to propose refined models and hypotheses pertaining to cardiac energy metabolism in the development of non-ischaemic heart failure. Protein structure-function analysis has been performed to evaluate contractile protein defects in inherited disorders; however, to date this approach has not been performed to directly address the role of energy utilization in the progression to heart failure. This strategy will therefore not be discussed further in this chapter.

1   Molecular genetics
2   Gene regulatory control
3   Genetic engineering (ablation/transgene)
4   Protein chemistry (structure/function analysis)

Figure 6-1. Molecular approaches in the evaluation of the development of disease.

MOLECULAR GENETICS OF HEART FAILURE

Familial analyses have shown that cardiomyopathy may have a genetic or inherited basis in children and adults. For example, approximately 20 percent of patients with idiopathic dilated cardiomyopathy were found to have a first-degree relative with myocardial dysfunction (Manolio et al, 1992). Many descriptions of individual kindreds with cardiomyopathy of unknown cause transmitted as autosomal dominant, autosomal recessive, and X-linked traits have appeared (Berko et al, 1987; Graber et al, 1986; Mestroni et al, 1990). Accordingly, a substantial proportion of idiopathic cardiomyopathies may have a genetic cause.

Molecular geneticists have concentrated primarily on identifying single-gene disorders resulting in human disease, including numerous cardiomyopathic syndromes. We recently reviewed the categories for which the genes causing cardiomyopathy have been identified (Kelly et al, 1994) (Table 6-1). Genetic defects have been predominantly identified in genes encoding cardiac contractile proteins. The identification of these gene defects, and the characterization of the encoded protein's functions are described in greater detail in the chapter by Watkins.

A second subset of genetic disorders include defects in genes encoding enzymes required for mitochondrial oxidative phosphorylation and for mitochondrial fatty acid β-oxidation. The majority of cardiomyopathy due to defects in mitochondrial oxidative phosphorylation are concurrent with neuromuscular defects or mitochondrial myopathies. Autosomal recessive defects in genes encoding multiple fatty acid β-oxidation enzymes cause cardiac hypertrophy, heart failure, and sudden death (Kelly et al, 1994). Moreover, in a recent study screening subjects with hereditary hypertrophic cardiomyopathy, a high incidence of a deficiency of a putative long chain fatty acid transporter (CD36) was noted in the subset of subjects with asymetrical hypertrophy of the cardiac septum. Furthermore, those individuals with deficiency in CD36 and asymmetrical septal hypertrophy also had decreased long chain fatty acid uptake into the hypertrophied myocardium despite normal myocardial perfusion (Tanaka et al, 1997). These data suggest that in a subset of subjects with genetic defects disrupting fatty acid metabolic genes, the reduced capacity to utilize fatty acids for energy production, can directly result in cardiac contractile dysfunction. However, whether a reduction in fatty acid utilization capacity, contributes to cardiac decompensation in acquired forms of heart disease are unknown.

Contractile/Structural Protein Gene Defects	Disorders of Energy Metabolism	X-Linked Muscular Dystrophies
Defects have been identified in genes encoding myosin heavy and light chain isoforms, troponin I and C isoforms, myosin binding protein C, and in α tropomyosin	Defects have been identified in genes encoding enzymes required for mitochondrial fatty acid uptake, β-oxidation and mitochondrial oxidative phosphorylation	Duchenne's and Becker's are the most common inherited skeletal myopathies. Defects have been identified in the gene encoding dystrophin, a large membrane associated protein in both syndromes.
The clinical features are variable, and include: asymmetrical septal hypertrophy, left ventricular hypertrophy, outflow tract obstruction. Sudden death is relatively common. Some subjects, however, are asymptomatic with or without ventricular hypertrophy	The clinical features of the fatty acid oxidation enzyme defects are variable, and include: cardiomyopathy, fasting hypoglycemia, hepatic dysfunction and skeletal myopathies. The clinical features of disorders in mitochondrial oxidative phosphorylation include: neuromuscular manifestations and mitochondrial myopathies. Skeletal myopathy is more common than the cardiac variant	The clinical features of both Duchenne's and Becker's muscular dystophy are predominantly skeletal myopathy. Most patients, however, have evidence of cardiomyopathy.

Table 6-1. Classification of inherited defects presenting with cardiomyopathy as a clinical feature. This classification is based on a review by Kelly et al., 1994, and summarizes the disorders. Disorders due to myocardial infiltration (e.g., glycogen storage diseases) are not reviewed.

GENE REGULATORY CONTROL

The study of inherited disorders resulting in cardiomyopathy discussed above has given us insight into potential mechanisms in the development of cardiac contractile function. To further enhance the understanding of the development of cardiac hypertrophy and the transition to heart failure, an approach would be to delineate and characterize the gene regulatory programmes activated during the development of these pathologies. Using this strategy, one can focus on cardiac gene/s known to be regulated by relevant pathologic cardiac stimuli such as pressure overload. Subsequently, the components of the pathway upstream of the candidate gene of interest can be characterized in "reverse" from the gene's promoter (on/off switch), to the promoter binding transcription factors (gene regulatory proteins), to intracellular signallers and finally to the membrane receptor and its ligand (Figure 6-2).

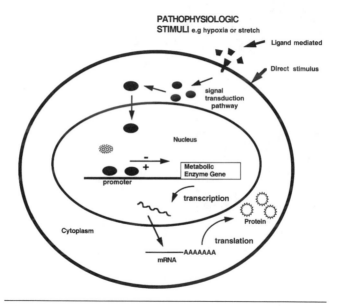

Figure 6-2. Schematic representation of a gene regulatory program in response to a pathophysiologic stimulus. The extracellar stimulus elicits a direct or a ligand/receptor-mediated response which couples to appropriate signal-transduction pathways. The intracellular signal transduction pathways activate specific transcription factors (regulatory proteins) to increase or decrease the transcription of target genes. These transcription factors bind to defined regions of the candidate genes promoter to modulate gene transcription. Translation of these genes result in the production of proteins in response to the initial extracellular stimulus.

The initial characterization would thus be at the level of the candidate gene's promoter. This structural region directs the expression of a gene in response to physiologic or pathologic signals (see Figure 6-2). The ability to understand the regulatory control of genes at the level of its promoter, has been vastly improved with the development of transgenic technology. This technology enables us to study a gene promoter's activity in the whole animal. Thus we can construct modified genes which include the candidate

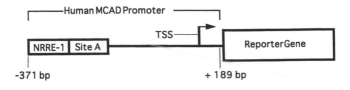

Figure 6-3. *Schematic representation of a transgene developed incorporating the human MCAD promoter and a reporter gene. The human MCAD promoter region from −371 base pairs (bp) upstream of the transcription start site (TSS) to + 189 bp downstream of the TSS is shown fused to an exogenous reporter gene. The reporter gene activity is a measure of the activity of the human MCAD promoter in-vivo. The nuclear receptor response element 1 (NRRE-1) and the GC nucleotide rich sequence (Site A) are two distinct regulatory regions of the promoter. The functional significance of these regulatory elements are discussed in the text.*

gene's promoter region fused to a reporter gene (see schematic diagram in Figure 6-3). These transgene constructs can be randomly inserted into the mouse genome. Measuring the activity of the reporter gene allows us to determine the ability of the incorporated promoter region to turn on (upregulate) or off (downregulate) the reporter in response to physiologic and pathologic stimuli in-vivo. Subsequent promoter region DNA:protein binding studies can be performed to identify the transcription factors that bind to the promoter and direct the appropriate regulation of the candidate gene.

This reverse approach has been used recently to elucidate adaptive and maladaptive responses of the cell during hypertrophy and in the failing heart (Reviewed, Kelly, 1994; Sack et al, 1998). We have used this reverse approach strategy, focusing on a gene encoding a rate-controlling energy substrate pathway enzyme.

THE MEDIUM CHAIN ACYL-COA DEHYDROGENASE GENE REGULATORY PROGRAMME

To begin to understand the role of disrupted fatty acid utilization in the development of heart failure, we have studied the gene regulatory programme of medium chain acyl-CoA dehydrogenase [MCAD; acyl-CoA:(acceptor)2,3-oxidoreductase, EC 1.3.99.3], a mitochondrial flavoenzyme that catalyzes the initial reaction in fatty acid β-oxidation (Beinert, 1963). We focused on the regulatory programme of this gene, as mutations in the MCAD gene are the most common inherited defect of the fatty acid utilization enzymes and a phenotypic presentation in individuals with defects in the MCAD gene includes cardiomyopathy (Kelly et al, 1994). Regulation of the MCAD gene was studied during cardiac development and with the onset of cardiac hypertrophy and heart failure. This strategy allowed us to determine that the expression of the MCAD gene is regulated coordinately with the known switch in energy substrate utilization during normal development and with the onset of cardiac pathology.

Cardiac developmental regulation

Expression of the MCAD gene is highly regulated among tissues and during development in accordance with substrate availability and cellular energy demands. MCAD mRNA and enzyme are expressed abundantly in the adult heart, in keeping with its reliance on oxidation of fatty acids for energy. During cardiac development, MCAD gene expression is induced in concert with the perinatal switch from glucose to fatty acids as the chief energy substrate (Kelly et al, 1989; Nagao et al, 1993). In the rat and mouse, this induction of MCAD mRNA levels is over 10-fold between the end of gestation and adulthood (Kelly et al, 1989; Disch et al, 1996).

To further characterize the gene regulatory mechanisms that control cellular fatty acid oxidative capacity, the human MCAD gene promoter has been extensively studied in-vitro (Carter et al, 1993 & 1994; Gulick et al, 1994; Leone et al, 1995; Raisher et al, 1992). The in-vitro studies identified MCAD promoter regions that appeared to play an important role in the regulation of the MCAD gene. Based on these data, we generated numerous transgenic mouse lines which included different regions of the human MCAD promoter and corresponding reporter genes (Disch et al, 1996). Studies were performed comparing the endogenous mouse MCAD expression and that of the human MCAD reporter gene activity during mouse development. A short region of the human MCAD promoter was identified, which is required for appropriate postnatal induction of MCAD gene expression in the heart. This promoter region is termed nuclear receptor response element 1 (NRRE-1), as regulatory proteins known as nuclear hormone receptor transcription factors, are known to bind to similar sequences in numerous gene promoters. These data indicate that the NRRE-1 promoter region of the human MCAD gene is required for the postnatal induction of MCAD gene expression in the heart during the transition from the reliance on glucose to fatty acids as the chief energy substrate. In addition, these data suggest that during cardiac development, MCAD gene expression is regulated in part at the level of gene transcription.

Cardiac hypertrophic regulation

The initial objective in evaluating the level of MCAD gene expression in cardiac hypertrophy was to assess whether this gene is regulated in parallel with the known alteration in myocardial energy substrate utilization in cardiac hypertrophy. We studied MCAD expression patterns in animal models with pressure and/or volume overload-induced cardiac hypertrophy (Sack et al, 1995 & 1996), and demonstrated a uniform and significant downregulation of this enzyme at the level of gene expression. These data suggested that the MCAD gene regulatory programme may be a useful target system to analyse with respect to alterations

.n cellular lipid metabolism during the development of cardiac hypertrophy and potentially with the transition to heart failure.

To assess whether the downregulation of MCAD in cardiac hypertrophy is regulated at the level of gene transcription, we evaluated whether the human MCAD gene promoter could repress the exogenous reporter gene activity in the previously generated transgenic mice (described above) during the induction of ventricular hypertrophy. A model of right ventricular hypertrophy induced via banding of the pulmonary artery, and compared to sham operated controls was used to study and compare the expression levels of the endogenous mouse MCAD and the human MCAD promoter driven reporter gene in response to ventricular hypertrophy. This mouse model has been well characterized and demonstrates appropriate molecular and physiologic alterations compatible with pressure overload-induced cardiac hypertrophy (Rockman et al, 1994). Our model induced profound right ventricular hypertrophy, with a more than doubling of the right ventricular mass compared to transgenic sham-control mice. The endogenous MCAD and transgene reporter mRNA levels were coordinately downregulated (> 75%) in the pressure overload right ventricles compared to the sham-operated right ventricles. In the transgenic animals harbouring a transgene excluding the NRRE-1 promoter region, endogenous MCAD mRNA expression was downregulated in parallel with the full length promoter transgenic mouse study, however, the transgene reporter activity was not downregulated in the hypertrophied ventricles. Taken together, these data indicate that the NRRE-1 promoter was indeed necessary for repression of MCAD gene transcription in the pressure overloaded ventricle. Accordingly, MCAD expression is downregulated at the transcriptional level in the hypertrophied myocardium, and the NRRE-1 promoter region is required as part of the hypertrophic responsive repressor regulatory elements in the human MCAD promoter.

Further experiments were performed to characterize the promoter regulatory region required for hypertrophic induced downregulation of MCAD gene expression. In brief, DNA:protein binding interaction studies were performed using various fragment lengths of the human MCAD promoter and nuclear protein extracts from hypertrophy and sham control right ventricular nuclear extracts. The most significant specific differential DNA:protein binding interactions between the two groups occurred at the NRRE-1 and an adjacent GC nucleotide rich promoter region [(Site A) — see schematic representation in Figure 6-3] of the human MCAD promoter. The NRRE-1 region has previously been implicated, as being required for hypertrophic MCAD gene regulation using the transgenic mice. The adjacent NRRE-1 and Site A regions are hence referred to as a hypertrophic responsive regulatory unit.

Antibody studies were performed to identify the regulatory proteins (transcription factors) which bind to this hypertrophic responsive regulatory unit, thereby potentially repressing MCAD gene transcription. Antibodies developed to recognize known cardiac enriched nuclear receptor and GC binding transcription factors (regulatory proteins that potentially bind to the DNA sequence of the hypertophy responsive regulatory unit) were analysed (Sack et al, 1997). Increased levels of the NRRE-1 binding transcription factor, chicken ovalbumin upstream promoter — transcription factor 1 (COUP-TF1) were present in the right ventricular hypertrophy mice nuclear extracts compared to control. COUP-TF1, is a recognized negative regulatory transcription factor (Carter et al, 1994). In addition, antibody studies using the GC rich site A promoter region as a probe identified increased levels of GC region binding transcription factors Sp1 and Sp3 in the right ventricular hypertrophy nuclear extracts compared to sham control ventricular nuclear extracts (schematic representation in Figure 3). These transcription factors have been described as having repressor activity (Li et al, 1996; Okumura et al, 1996). These data identified nuclear regulatory proteins which bind to the human MCAD promoter hypertrophic responsive regulatory unit, and potentially play a role in repressing MCAD gene expression in response to ventricular pressure overload.

The MCAD gene regulatory program reverts to the fetal gene programme during cardiac hypertrophy

Numerous investigators have demonstrated, while studying the molecular regulatory events associated with cardiac hypertrophy, that there is a re-expression of the foetally enriched isoforms of numerous genes encoding cardiac contractile and ion regulatory proteins (Reviewed, Schwartz, et al 1992 and Sack et al, 1998). The current paradigm therefore suggests that: activation of the "foetal gene" programme is likely to be an adaptive structural and metabolic response of the overloaded ventricle to maximize chemomechanical energy conversion efficiency, and thereby decrease oxygen consumption in the hypertrophied heart. This reversion to the expression of foetal isoforms is paralleled at the metabolic level in the switch in energy substrate utilization in the heart with the development of cardiac hypertrophy and failure. The data presented above suggests that at the level of gene expression, MCAD parallels the known metabolic pertubations and returns to foetal expression levels with the development of cardiac hypertrophy.

To determine whether the downregulation of MCAD expression during cardiac hypertrophy is due to reactivation of a foetal gene regulatory programme, the DNA:protein binding and associated antibody identification experiments were repeated using nuclear extracts isolated from developing foetal hearts. The results obtained were compared to the studies using the normal adult and hypertrophied adult heart nuclear extracts. The DNA:protein binding interactions were similar between the foetal and right ventricular hypertrophy cardiac nuclear extracts, and, the transcription factors identified as being upregulated in hypertrophy were increased in parallel in the foetal nuclear extracts (Sack, et al 1997). These data suggest that the repression of MCAD gene expression with cardiac hypertrophy involves reactivation of foetal transcriptional control mechanisms at the hypertrophy responsive unit incorporating NRRE-1 and Site A (see schematic in Figure 3).

Regulatory control of MCAD in the transition from compensated cardiac hypertrophy to the decompensated failing heart

To determine whether MCAD was differentially regulated in the hypertrophied and failing heart, we studied MCAD gene expression, protein levels and enzyme activity in a rat model with a well characterized temporal progression from the normal heart to compensated hypertrophy and ultimately to decompensated heart failure. The SHHF/Mcc^{facp} (SHHF) rat strain is a genetically inbred strain that develops hypertension, hypertrophy and congestive heart failure (McCune et al, 1991 and 1995; Park et al, 1996). The levels of mRNA encoding MCAD was significantly lower in the hypertrophied and failing rat left ventricles compared to control. No significant difference of the MCAD gene expression was seen between the hypertrophied and failing ventricles (Sack et al, 1996). These data indicate that expression of MCAD is downregulated at the pre-translational level in parallel with known alterations in myocardial energy substrate in the hypertrophied and failing SHHF rat ventricle. Moreover, no significant difference in MCAD gene expression levels were detected between the left ventricular hypertrophy and heart failure ventricular tissue. In contrast to MCAD mRNA levels, mean immunodetectable steady-state MCAD protein levels in the hypertrophied rats were not significantly different than the control rat levels. However, in the heart failure group, MCAD mRNA and protein levels were coordinately and significantly downregulated to a similar degree. In addition, MCAD enzymatic activities paralleled protein levels during the transition from left ventricular hypertrophy to heart failure (Figure 6-4) (Sack et al, 1996). These findings have identified a discordance between MCAD mRNA levels and the protein and enzyme activity levels during the hypertrophy stage of this rat model and suggests that translational or post-translational regulatory mechanisms are involved in the maintenance of MCAD expression in compensated left ventricular hypertrophy. This data does not distinguish between the role of decreased fatty acid β-oxidation enzyme expression as a primary event in promoting the transition from compensated ventricular hypertrophy to overt heart failure versus a secondary phenomenon.

MCAD gene regulation in human idiopathic dilated cardiomyopathy

The data described above indicate that the expression of a gene encoding a mitochondrial β-oxidation enzyme is downregulated in parallel with known alterations in energy substrate utilization during the development of experimental heart failure. We sought to determine whether MCA

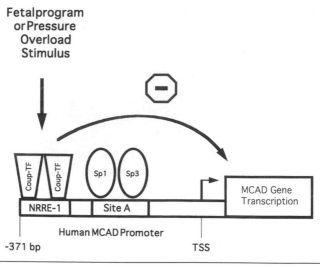

Figure 6-4. *Proposed foetal and hypertrophic induced transcriptional repression of MCAD gene expression. A schematic representation of the results from the DNA:protein binding studies. These implicate that the binding of the transcription factors — COUP-TF, Sp1 and Sp3, to the NRRE-1/SiteA hypertrophic responsive regulatory unit repress MCAD gene expression during fetal development and with the induction of cardiac hypertorphy. TSS — transcription start site.*

levels and activity were downregulated in human heart failure. Tissue samples were obtained from the ventricles of human cardiac transplant recipients with severe idiopathic dilated cardiomyopathy. The results were compared to age-matched normal control hearts obtained at postmortem. MCAD protein, enzyme activity and mRNA levels were characterized in the cardiomyopathy and control ventricles. Compared to control levels, mean MCAD protein levels, enzyme activity and mRNA levels were significantly

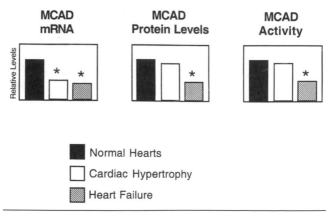

Figure 6-5. *Comparison of MCAD mRNA, MCAD protein and MCAD enzymatic activity levels in control, hypertrophied and failing SHHF rat hearts. Solid bars indicate normal cardiac levels (control), open bars cardiac hypertrophy levels and hatched bars cardiomyopathic heart levels. MCAD mRNA and immunodetectable protein values are normalized to corresponding control values. Steady-state MCAD protein levels were determined by immunoblot analysis of protein extracts prepared from the same ventricular samples used for isolation of total RNA. The asterisks represents a p value < 0.05 compared to the corresponding control values.*

reduced in the ventricles of subjects with idiopathic dilated cardiomyopathy (Sack et al, 1996). Thus, as demonstrated for the rat heart failure models, left ventricular MCAD is downregulated in this group of patients with human dilated cardiomyopathy at the pre-translational level.

These data parallel known alterations in myocardial energy substrate in some subjects with failing ventricles. The reduced MCAD protein levels and enzyme activity in the cardiomyopathy subjects compared to controls parallel those found in the SHHF rat model and suggest a similar translational or post-translational regulatory program between human idiopathic dilated cardiomyopathy and heart failure resulting from pressure overload in the SHHF rat.

GENETIC ENGINEERING (THE GENE TARGETTING APPROACH)

Gene targetting by homologous recombination has rapidly become a common method to analyse gene function and to develop animal models of disease. Gene targetting is based on homologous DNA recombination, a reaction whereby a DNA fragment introduced into the nucleus of a cell can be specifically integrated into the homologous (exact) genomic position, thus replacing the homologus (natural) gene. When this process is carried out in mouse embryonic stem cells, a transgenic mouse can be generated by injecting the stem cells into a mouse embryo at the blastocyst stage. The number of mutant mouse strains generated by this approach has skyrocketed after the seminal contribution of Manhsour et al. (1988), showing that homologous recombination can be attained and detected at virtually any locus in the mouse genome.

Using this approach, a candidate gene can be disrupted in the mouse genome. The loss of function of the protein encoded by this candidate gene may give us insight into the functional role of this protein in-vivo. Therefore, ablation of a gene encoding a rate-controlling metabolic enzyme may give us insight into the functional significance of disrupting that metabolic pathways in the development of cardiac pathology. To illustrate this methodological approach, the deletion of a gene encoding a key cardiac enriched glucose transporter, thought to be important in the development of non-insulin dependent diabetes will be reviewed.

GLUCOSE TRANSPORTER GENE DISRUPTION AND THE DEVELOPMENT OF CARDIAC HYPERTROPHY

Background

With the development of cardiac hypertrophy, aerobic glycolysis from exogenous glucose is accelerated (Allard et al., 1994; Schonekess et al., 1995). The uptake of exogenous glucose is regulated by the transmembrane gradient and by the concentration and activity of the facilitative glucose transporters. Two isoforms of the glucose transporter family have been identified in the myocardium. GLUT1, the more ubiquitous isoform, is thought to be the major determinant of basal glucose transport in cardiac muscle (Laybutt et al., 1997). GLUT4 is the predominant cardiac adult isoform and and is highly regulated during acute cardiac stress (DaQuing et al., 1994). GLUT4 is in addition, insulin-responsive and highly regulated at the pre- and post-translational levels (Kraegen et al, 1993; Slot et al., 1991; Tebbey et al., 1994). The process of insulin-stimulated glucose uptake is defective in the muscle of patients with type II diabetes (Rothman et al., 1992) and so there is considerable interest in the mechanism of GLUT4 activation and the establishment of methods by which this "insulin-resistance" can be overcome. Thus, the ablation of the GLUT4 gene was undertaken by homologous recombination [(GLUT4-/-), (Katz et al., 1995)] to determine the developmental and metabolic consequences of abolishing the most abundant glucose transporter in insulin target tissues including the heart.

Mice deficient in GLUT4 develop cardiac hypertrophy

The mice deficient in GLUT4 are growth-retarded, experience decreased longevity, develop cardiac hypertrophy and exhibit severely reduced adipose tissue deposits. In addition, these mice exhibited postprandial hyperinsulinemia, indicating possible insulin resistance and increased expression of cardiac GLUT1. The authors conclude that functional GLUT4 protein is essential for sustained growth, normal cellular glucose and fat metabolism, and expected longevity (Katz, et al. 1995). The significant cardiac hypertrophy in these GLUT4 null mice is thought to be due to the hyperinsulinemia (growth factor mediated) in these animals, and/or the decreased supply of free fatty acids to the heart. Importantly, insulin-resistance has been described in hypertensive and failing heart conditions (Pasternostro et al., 1996; Swan et al., 1994). Likewise, reduced free fatty acid utilization by the heart as exhibited via pharmacologic inhibition of fatty acid b-oxidation (Greaves et al., 1984; Bressler et al., 1989; Rupp et al., 1992) as well as the genetic defects described above are known to induce cardiac hypertrophy. The mechanisms of these phenomena are, however, unknown. Further characterization of the GLUT4 deficient mice has suggested that another probable hypertrophic inducing factor is the development of hypertension in the heterozygous knockout GLUT4 mice [(GLUT4+/-), (Stenbit et al., 1997)].

GLUT4 expression reverts to the fetal pattern during the induction of cardiac hypertrophy

Interestingly, as with the fatty acid utilizing enzyme genes, GLUT4 is highly regulated during development, with low expression in the fetal and neonatal stages, and high expres-

.on in the adult myocardium (Postic et al., 1994). We .unpublished data) and others have demonstrated that at the level of gene expression and whole cell protein levels, GLUT4 reverts to fetal levels with the development of pressure overload-induced cardiac hypertrophy (Pasternostro et al., 1995). This seems counterintuitive, as GLUT4 is the predominant cardiac glucose transporter, and glucose utilization is known to be increased in cardiac hypertrophy. The metabolic substrate utilization studies in the GLUT4 ablation studies described above, however, demonstrate that despite a complete absence of GLUT4, glucose uptake and utilization are increased in the hypertrophic GLUT4 deficient mice compared to normal controls (Chatham et al., 1998) (Table 6-2). In these studies, the level of GLUT1 is augmented and probably overcompensates for the loss of GLUT4 (Katz et al., 1995).

The phenomenon of the reversion to the fetal gene regulatory program, is however evident with respect to glucose transport in pressure-overload induced cardiac hypertrophy. Thus the paradigm of reversion to the fetal gene programme as previously demonstrated in contractile and ion regulatory control probably can be extended to the control of energy metabolism in the heart.

Table 6-2. Phenotypic characteristics of the GLUT4 null and heterozygous ablation mice.

Gene Ablation	Neurohormonal/Metabolic Manifestations	Cardiac Phenotype
GLUT4 Disruption	Insulin Resistance	Cardiac Hypertrophy
	Hypertension	Diabetic Histopathology
	Altered fatty acid metabolism Increased glucosed uptake	

The functional contribution of the metabolic, neurohormonal and haemodynamic pertubations to the development of cardiac hypertrophy in these mice are speculative at this time.

CONCLUSIONS AND PERSPECTIVES

Studying the fatty acid β-oxidation enzyme gene regulatory programme suggests complex molecular regulatory events that are activated with the induction of cardiac growth and further regulated in parallel with the transition from the compensated hypertrophic to the decompensated failing heart. These alterations in cardiac metabolic gene regulation are consistent with previous observations that energy derived from fatty acid oxidation is reduced in the hypertrophied and failing heart, with an increase in the utilization of glucose substrates. Transcriptional repression of MCAD gene expression via reactivation of a fetal gene regulatory programme is evident after a short term pressure-load on the heart, as seen in our transgenic mouse study. The MCAD levels and activity are maintained near baseline in the SHHF rat ventricle as long as the heart is compensated with good contractile function. The onset of heart failure is characterized by a reduction in the MCAD enzyme levels and activity, in parallel with the gene expression pattern. Of note, in this study we were not able to distinguish the temporal relationship between fatty acid b-oxidation enzyme gene downregulation and the onset of myocyte hypertrophy, nor between the sequence of reduced fatty acid β-oxidation enzyme levels and activity and the onset of myocyte decompensation. However, we believe that this regulatory pathway represents a useful target for future experimental studies aimed at characterization of alterations in cellular lipid metabolism during myocyte growth and may contribute to the determination of the functional role of energy utilization in the transition from cardiac hypertrophy to heart failure. The pathological significance of reduced fatty acid utilization in cardiac decompensation remains speculative. However, with the advancement in the field, we believe that the working hypothesis can be refined. Thus, we hypothesize that the energy substrate preference switch during cardiac hypertrophy is initially an adaptive gene regulatory programme within the framework of the reactivation of the fetal gene regulatory program. Moreover, we hypothesize that this gene regulatory programme becomes maladaptive, potentially at a post-transcriptional level, thereby contributing to cardiac decompensation and resultant heart failure.

In concert with the molecular regulation of the fatty acid β-oxidation enzyme genes in acquired cardiac haemodynamic overload, GLUT4 downregulation is probably due to the reactivation of the fetal gene regulatory programme. Moreover, the phenotypic characterization, metabolic profiles and haemodynamic pertubations delineated in the GLUT4 ablation mice studies have suggested an additional mechanisms with respect to the contribution of cardiac metabolism to the development of cardiac hypertrophy and the transition to heart failure. These include the resultant development of neurohormonal aberations associated with the alteration in energy metabolic genes as evidenced by hyperinsulinemia (insulin resistance) (Rossetti et al., 1997), the reduced fatty acid metabolism (Chatham et al., 1998) and the elevated blood pressure in the GLUT4 defective mice.

The data presented with respect to molecular regulatory control of energy metabolic pathways strongly suggests that the identification of the molecular triggers involved in reactivating the cardiac fetal gene regulatory programme are pivotal to the understanding and thus prevention of the decompensation of the myocardial contractile apparatus. This enhanced understanding will allow us to ultimately design strategies/therapies to prevent the transition to contractile failure in the overloaded non-ischaemic heart. Moreover, utilizing modern molecular approaches, combining molecular genetics, the study of gene regulatory control and gene ablation technology will allow us to ultimately define the functional significance of energy substrate switches in cardiac contractile decompensation.

REFERENCES

Allard MF, Schonekess B, Henning SL, English DR, Lopaschuck GD. Contribution of oxidative metabolism and glycolysis to ATP production in hypertrophied hearts. *Am J Physiol.* 1994; 267:H742–H750.

Beinert, H. In *The Enzymes*, eds. Boyer PD, Lardy H, Myrback K. (Academic, New York), 1963; Vol. 7:447–476.

Bellamy N, Duffy D, Martin N, Mathews J. Rheumatoid arthritis in twins. *Ann Rheum. Dis.* 1992; 51:588–593.

Berko BA, Swift M. X-linked dilated cardiomyopathy. *N. Engl J Med* 1987; 316:1186–1191.

Bressler R, Gay R, Copeland JG, Bahl JJ, Bedotto J, Goldman S. Chronic inhibition of fatty acid oxidation: new model of diastolic dysfunction. *Life Sci.* 1989; 44: 1897–1906.

Carter ME, Gulick T, Raisher BD, Caira T, Ladias JAA, Moore DD, Kelly DP. Hepatocyte nuclear factor-4 activates medium chain acyl-CoA dehydrogenase gene transcription by interacting with a complex regulatory element. *J. Biol. Chem.* 1993; 268:13805–13810.

Carter ME, Gulick TG, Moore DD, Kelly DP. A pleiotropic element in the medium-chain acyl coenzyme A dehydrogenase gene promoter mediates transcriptional regulation by multiple nuclear receptor transcription factors and defines novel receptor-DNA binding motifs. *Mol. Cell. Biol.* 1994; 14: 4360–4372.

Chatham JC, Chacko VP, Charron MJ, Katz EB, Ocampo C, Weiss RG. Myocardial metabolism in the GLUT4 knockout mouse. *J. Mol. Cell. Cardiol.* In Press.

Christe ME, Rodgers RL. Altered glucose and fatty acid oxidation in hearts of the spontaneously hypertensive rat. *J. Mol. Cell. Cardiol.* 1994; 26:1371–1375.

DaQing S, Ngoc N, DeGrado TR, Schwaiger M, Brosius FC. Ischemias induces translocation of the insulin-responsive glucose transporter GLUT4 to the plasma membrane of cardiac myocytes. *Circulation* 1994; 89:793–798.

Disch DL, Rader TA, Cresci S, Leone TC, Barger PM, Vega R, Wood PA, Kelly DP. Transcriptional control of a nuclear gene encoding a mitochondrial fatty acid oxidation enzyme in transgenic mice: role for nuclear receptors in cardiac and brown adipose tissue expression. *Mol. Cell. Biol.* 1996; 16: 4043–4051.

Graber HL, Unverferth DV, Baker PB, Ryan JM, Baba N, Wooley CF. Evolution of a hereditary cardiac conduction and muscle disorder: a study involving a family with six generations affected. *Circulation* 1986; 74:21–35.

Greaves P, Martin J, Michel, MC, Mompon P. Cardiac hypertrophy in the dog and rat induced by oxfenicine, an agent which modifies muscle metabolism. *Arch. Toxicol.* 1984; 7: 488–493.

Gulick T, Cresci S, Caira T, Moore DD, Kelly DP. The peroxisome proliferator-activated receptor regulates mitochondrial fatty acid oxidative enzyme gene expression. *Proc. Natl. Acad. Sci. USA* 1994; 91:11012–11016.

Feinendegen LE, Henrich MM, Kuikka JT, Thompson KH, Vester EG, Strauer B. Myocardial lipid turnover in dilated cardiomyopathy: A dual in vivo tracer approach. *J. Nucl. Cardiol.* 1995; 2:42–52.

Ingwall JS. Is cardiac failure a consequence of decreased energy reserve? *Circulation* 1993; 87[suppl VII]:VII-58–VII-62.

Katz AM. Cellular mechanisms in congestive heart failure. *Am Cardiol.* 1988; 62:3A–8A.

Katz EB, Stenbit AE, Hatton K, DePinho R, Charron MJ. Cardiac and adipose tissue abnormalities but not diabetes in mice deficient in GLUT4. *Nature* 1995; 377:151–155.

Kelly DP, Gordon JI, Strauss AW. The tissue-specific expression and developmental regulation of two nuclear genes encoding rat mitochondrial proteins: medium-chain acyl-CoA dehydrogenase adn mitochondrial malate dehydrogenase. *J. Biol. Chem.* 1989; 264:18921–18925.

Kelly DP, Strauss AW. Inherited cardiomyopathies. *N. Engl. J. Med.* 1994; 330:913–919.

Kelly DP. Current concepts of the molecular basis of heart failure. *Coronary Artery Disease* 1994; 5:873–875.

Kraegen EW, Sowden JA, Halstead MB, Clark PW, Rodnick KJ, Chisholm DJ, James, DE. Glucose transporters and in vivo glucose uptake in skeletal and cardiac muscle: fasting, insulin stimulation and immunolocalization studies of GLUT1 and GLUT4. *Biochem J.* 1993; 295:287–293.

Laybutt DR, Thompson AL, Cooney GJ, Kraegen EW. Selective chronic regulation of GLUT1 and GLUT4 content by insulin, glucose, and lipid in rat cardiac muscle in vivo. *Am. J. Physiol.* 1997; 273:H1309–H1316.

Leone TC, Cresci S, Carter ME, Zhang Z, Lala DS, Strauss AW, Kelly DP. The human medium chain acyl-CoA dehydrogenase gene promoter consists of a complex arrangement of nuclear receptor response elements and Sp1 binding sites. *J. Biol. Chem.* 1995; 270:16309–16314.

Li R, Hodny Z, Luciakova K, Barath P, Nelson BD. Sp1 activates and inhibits transcription from separate elements in the proximal promoter of the human adenine nucleotide translocase 2 (ANT2) gene. *J. Biol. Chem.* 1996; 271:18925–18930.

Manolio TA, Baughman KL, Rodeheffer R, et al. Prevalence and etiology of idiopathic dilated cardiomyopathy (summary of a National Heart, Lung, and Blood Institute workshop). *Am J Cardiol* 1992; 69:1458–1466.

Mansour SL, Thomas KR, Capecchi MR. Disruption of the proto-oncogene int-2 in mouse embryo-derived stem cells: a general strategy for targeting mutations to non-selectable genes. *Nature* 1988; 336:348–352.

McCune SA, Jenkins JE, Stills HF, Jr., Park S, Radin MJ, Jurin RR, Hamlin RE. Renal and heart function in the SHHF/Mcc-cp rat. In *Frontiers in Diabetes Research.* Lessons from Animal Diabetes III. Shafrir E, editor. Smith-Gorden, 1991; 397–401.

McCune SA, Park S, Radin MJ, Jurin RR. The SHHF/Mcc-facp: A genetic model of congestive heart failure. In *Mechanisms of Heart Failure.* Singal PK, Dixon IMC, Beamish RE, and Dhalla NS, Eds. Kluwer Academic Publishers, Boston, MA. 1995; 8:91–106.

Mestroni L, Miani D, Di Lenarda A, et al. Clinical and pathologic study of familial dilated cardiomyopathy. *Am J Cardiol* 1990; 65:1449–1453.

Okumura K, Sakaguchi G, Takagi S, Naito K, Mimori T, Igarashi H. Sp1 family proteins recognize the U5 repressive element of the long terminal repeat of the human T cell leukemia virus type I through binding to the CACCC core motif. *J. Biol. Chem.* 1996; 271:12944–12950.

Park SC, Leszczynski J, McCune SA, Bonagura JD. Echocardiographic studies of progression to congestive heart failure in lean male SHHF/Mcc-facp rats. *FASEB* 10:A345, 1996 (Abstract).

Pasternostro G, Clarke K, Heath J, Seymour AML, Radda GK. Decreased GLUT-4 content and insulin-sensitive deoxyglucose uptake show insulin resistance in the hypertensive rat heart. *Cardiovascular Research*. 1995; 30:205–211.

Pasternostro G, Camici PG, Lammerstma AA, Marinho N, Baliga RR, Kooner JS, Radda GK, Ferrannini E. Cardiac and skeletal muscle insulin resistance in patients with coronary heart disease. A study with positron emission tomography. *J. Clin. Invest.* 1996; 98:2094–2099.

Postic C, Leturque A, Printz RL, Maulard P, Loizeau M, Granner DK, Girard J. Development and regulation of glucose transporter and hexokinase expression in rat. *Am J Physiol* 1994; 266:E548–E559.

Raisher BD, Gulick T, Zhang Z, Strauss AW, Moore DD, Kelly DP. Identification of a novel retinoid-responsive element in the promoter region of the medium chain acyl-CoA dehydrogenase gene. *J. Biol. Chem.* 1992; 267:20264–20269.

Rockman HA, Ono S, Ross RS, Jones LR, Karimi M, Bhargava V, Ross J, Chien KR. Molecular and physiological alterations in murine ventricular dysfunction. *Proc. Natl. Acad. Sci. USA* 1994; 91: 2694–2698.

Rossetti L, Stenbit AE, Chen W, Hu M, Barzilai N, Katz EB, Charron MJ. Peripheral but not hepatic insulin resistance in mice with one disrupted allele of the glucose transporter type 4 (GLUT4) gene. *J. Clin. Invest.* 1997; 100:1831–1839.

Rothman-DL; Shulman-RG; Shulman-GI. 31P nuclear magnetic resonance measurements of muscle glucose-6-phosphate. Evidence for reduced insulin-dependent muscle glucose transport or phosphorylation activity in non-insulin-dependent diabetes mellitus. *J-Clin-Invest*. 1992; 89:1069–75.

Rupp H, Jacob R. Metabolically-modulated growth and phenotype of the rat. *Eur. Heart J.* 1992; 13: 56–61.

Sack MN, Johnson CM, Pogwizd SM, Kelly DP. Regulation of mitochondrial fatty acid oxidation enzyme gene expression in the failing heart. *J. Mol. Cell. Cardiol.* 1995; 27:A58.

Sack MN, Rader TA, Park S, Bastin J, McCune SA, Kelly DP. Fatty acid oxidation enzyme gene expression is downregulated in the failing heart. *Circulation.* 1996; 94:2837–2842.

Sack MN, Disch DL, Rockman HA, Kelly DP. A role for Sp and nuclear receptor transcription factors in a cardiac hypertrophy program. *Proc. Natl. Acad. Sci. USA* 1997; 94:6438–6443.

Sack MN, Kelly DP. The energy substrate switch during the development of heart failure: Gene regulatory mechanisms. *Int. J. Mol. Med.* — 1998; 1:17–24.

Scheuer J. Metabolic factors in myocardial failure. *Circulation* 1993; 87[suppl VII]:VII-54–VII-57.

Schonekess B, Allard MF, Lopaschuk GD. Propionyl L-carnitine improvement of hypertrophied rat heart function is associated with increase in cardiac efficiency. *Eur J Pharmacol.* 1995; 286:155–166.

Schonekess B, Allard MF, Lopaschuk GD. Propionyl L-carnitine improvement of hypertrophied heart function is accompanied by an increase in carbohydrate oxidation. *Circ Res.* 1995; 77:726–734.

Schwartz K, Boheler K, de la Bastie D, Lompre AM, Mercadier JJ. Switches in cardiac muscle gene expression as a result of pressure and volume overload. *Am. J. Physiol.* 1992; 262:R364–R369.

Slot JW, Geuze HJ, Gigengack S, James DE, Lienhard GE. Translocation of the glucose transporter GLUT4 in cardiac myocytes in the rat. *Proc Natl Acad Sci, USA.* 1991; 88:7815–7819.

Stenbit AE, Tsao TS, Li J, Burcelin R, Greenen DL, Factor SM, Houseknecht K, Katz EB, Charron MJ. GLUT4 heterozygous knockout mice develop muscle insulin resistance and diabetes. *Nature Medicine* 1997; 3:1096–1101.

Swan JW, Walton C, Godsland IF, Clark AL, Coats AJ, Oliver MF. Insulin resistance in chronic heart failure. *Eur. Heart J.* 1994; 15:1528–1532.

Tanaka T, Sohmiya K, Kawamura K. Is CD36 deficiency an etiology of hereditary hypertrophic cardiomyopathy? *J. Mol. Cell. Cardiol.* 1997; 29:121–127.

Tebbey PW, McGowan KM, Stephens JM, Buttke TM, Pekala PH. Arachidonic acid down-regulates the insulin-dependent glucose transporter (GLUT4) in 3T3-Li adipocytes by inhibiting transcription and enhancing mRNA turnover. *J. Biol. Chem.* 1994; 269:639–644.

CHAPTER 7

Left Ventricular Hypertrophy at the Limits

George A. Mensah

INTRODUCTION

Left ventricular hypertrophy (LVH) is a powerful predictor of cardiovascular morbidity and mortality. Traditionally viewed as a physiological response to an increase in systemic hemodynamic load, LVH begins as a structural adaptation designed to match heart size and shape to the type and severity of hemodynamic load. This architectural remodelling is quantitatively and qualitatively heterogeneous and often becomes mismatched to the inciting hemodynamic stimulus leading to adverse consequences. It is not surprising, therefore, that the presence of LVH, even when mild, is a major independent marker of fatal and non-fatal cardiovascular events as well as death from all causes in both men and women (Levy et al. 1990; Koren et al. 1991). At the limits of the hypertrophic process, heart failure ensues with both diastolic and systolic impairment, thereby predisposing the individual to premature cardiovascular mortality.

In this chapter, LVH is defined and the important distinction between physiological and pathological LVH is emphasized. The anatomical, physiological and clinical determinants, and limits of LVH are reviewed. The role of genetic and hereditary predisposition is discussed and the limits of LVH in health and disease are outlined. The biological and epidemiological relevance of these limits and their implications for the evaluation and management of cardiovascular disease are also discussed. The merits and limitations of the published data on the beneficial effects of LVH regression and the role of antihypertensive interventions are reviewed. Finally, important future perspectives and novel concepts regarding gene expression in cardiac hypertrophy and the intentional induction of cardiac hypertrophy for the treatment of cardiovascular disease are discussed.

PHYSIOLOGICAL AND PATHOLOGICAL HYPERTROPHY

Left ventricular hypertrophy as an initially useful physiological adaptation to conditions of increasing metabolic and hemodynamic load is well recognized. In this "physiologi-cal hypertrophy", as seen in normal growth and increased regular physical exercise, the normal cardiac ultrastructural architecture is preserved. In addition, the normal relation-ship between myocyte and non-myocyte tissue is main-tained. This results because the increase in individual myocyte size and myocardial bulk is accompanied by a proportionate increase in the size of non-myocyte cells and bulk of extracellular tissue. There is no evidence that this physiological LVH is associated with adverse prognosis.

In contrast, "pathological hypertrophy" carries a grim prognosis. By definition, pathological hypertrophy is seen in disease states or in the setting of increased release of fac-tors associated with abnormal cardiac physiology, overex-pression of proto-oncogenes, and certain genetic mutations. Typically, cardiac structure and function are abnormal. Even in the absence of gross structural abnormalities, the normal relationship between myocyte and non-myocyte cells is perturbed. There is often an excess of collagen and extracellular matrix so that diastolic cardiac properties become abnormal when systolic function remains normal or increased. LVH in this setting always identifies affected individuals as high risk for premature fatal and non-fatal cardiovascular events. The elusive factors and signals that transform an initially physiological adaptation into an adverse prognostic marker remain important research sub-jects. This chapter deals predominantly with the limits of this pathological LVH.

ANATOMICAL LIMITS

Normal Limits of LV Mass:

Continued architectural remodelling, comprising myocyte hypertrophy rather than hyperplasia, matches heart size to hemodynamic load and metabolic needs associated with normal growth. Since metabolic needs are determined lar-gely by body size and physical activity, heart size is impor-tantly influenced by measures of physical build such as body weight, lean body mass and body height as well as the level of physical exercise. The normal limits to left ven-tricular (LV) mass in healthy adults are therefore deter-mined by body height, body weight, lean body mass and cardiac stroke work. The powerful curvilinear relationship between body height and LV mass in normotensive, nor-mal-weight subjects ranging in age from infancy to adult-hood is shown in Figure 7-1. Data from autopsy studies show that normal LV weight is less than 175 g in normal adults of average body build and rarely exceed 215 g in those of large build or increased physical activity (Bove et al. 1966). Normal values for the whole heart average 325 g and 275 g in adult men and women, respectively. When expressed as a percentage of body weight, normal limits of heart weight in healthy adults have been estimated as 0.4–0.45%.

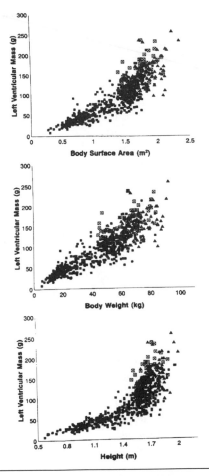

Figure 7-1. The powerful curvilinear relationship between body height and LV mass in normotensive, normal-weight subjects aged 4 months through 72 years. (Reprinted from de Simone et al. 1992; with permission)

The availability of autopsy-validated echocardiographic methods (Devereux and Roman, 1995) have permitted systematic evaluation of the clinically meaningful parameters necessary for reliable assessment of the limits of normal LV mass. In Table 7-1, the upper normal limits for total LV mass and LV mass indexed by height, height$^{2.7}$, body surface area according to sex-independent and gender-specific criteria are summarized. Absolute heart weights and LV mass indexes are greater in men than in women. However,

TABLE 7-1: CRITERIA FOR DIAGNOSIS OF LVH ON ECHOCARDIOGRAPHY

Criterion	Male	Female	Either Sex	Reference
LVM/BSA (g/m2)	134	109	–	Devereux et al. 1984
	131	100	-	Savage et al. 1987
	–	–	125	Koren et al. 1991
LVM/Height (g/m)	143	102	–	Levy et al. 1987
	126	105	–	De Simone et al. 1995
LVM/ Height$^{2.7}$ (g/m$^{2.7}$)	50	47	–	De Simone et al. 1992
	–	–	51	De Simone et al. 1995

the prevalence of LVH is higher in women than in men when either single partition values or gender-specific criteria are used to define LVH. This likely reflects a mortality selection with greater premature mortality in men with LVH. Although gender influences the normal limits of LV mass, age and blood pressure level in the normal range do not significantly affect these limits (Devereux and Roman, 1995). In the very elderly however, LVH is commonly seen. In a review of 237 autopsy cases in patients who had lived 90 years and older, Lie and Hammond (1988) noted that the heart weight ranged from 235 to 640 g (mean, 405 g) in the 93 men and 200 to 740 g (mean, 355 g) in the 144 women. The mean heart weight of 0.6% of mean body weight was significantly higher than the corresponding value of 0.4-0.45% in younger persons (Eckner et al. 1969). In these very senescent individuals, the most common cause of death (in 48% of cases) was cardiovascular disease — an important cause of increased heart weight (Hodkinson et al. 1979).

Race and LVH

Although race or ethnicity is often cited as an important determinant of LVH, the data are inconclusive when echocardiographically-determined LV mass or mass index criteria are used for defining LVH. In addition, the concept of race as a biologic variable has not usually been rigorously dealt with (Cooper, 1984) so that where differences are noted, it is uncertain if they reflect "racial" differences or environmental, cultural, socioeconomic, or other variable commonly seen in the respective ethnic communities. In addition, rarely are studies adequately matched for total burden of hypertension or even family history of hypertension. Nevertheless, the published data in Black and White subjects in the United States suggest that ECG evidence of LVH may be as much as ten-fold greater in Blacks (Sutherland, 1993). These reports were important because they suggested a possibility that the greater prevalence of LVH might explain the disproportionate excess of cardiovascular mortality in Blacks (Koren et al. 1993; Mayet et al. 1994). More recently however, Lee et al. (1992) have shown that conventional ECG criteria overestimate the Black–White differences in LVH prevalence. In general, there have been as many reports of a greater prevalence as there are of a no difference in prevalence when echocardiographic LV mass criteria are used for LVH definition in Blacks and Whites. There is more consistency in a finding of greater septal and relative wall thickness in black compared to white patients (Koren et al. 1993; Hammond et al. 1984; Liebson et al. 1993; Lee et al. 1993).

Thus, the anatomic limits to LVH in healthy persons appear to be influenced by body weight, body height, gender and to a lesser extent, age, physical activity and level of blood pressure within the normal range. The evidence for an *independent effect* of race on the prevalence and severity of LVH remains inconclusive.

The Limits of LV Mass in Disease States

Although blood pressure level within the normal range does not significantly affect LV mass limits, the presence of chronic arterial hypertension commonly leads to LVH. Even in the setting of relatively uncomplicated mild to moderate hypertension, LVH may be detected by echocardiography in 12–30% in unselected patients (Hammond et al. 1986, Devereux et al. 1987, Levy et al. 1988, Laufer et al. 1989, Liebson et al. 1993) and up to 60% of adult hypertensives referred to tertiary care and specialized hypertension centres (Savage et al. 1979, Devereux et al. 1983a, Devereux et al. 1983b, Abi-Samra et al. 1983). LVH may be seen in up to 90% of patients with chronic severe or malignant hypertension (Shapiro et al. 1981, Messerli et al. 1983). Thus, severity and chronicity significantly affect the prevalence of LVH in hypertensive adults. Other important parameters that affect the prevalence of LVH in hypertension include obesity, gender and possibly age (Devereux and Roman, 1995).

In addition to hypertension, the major etiologies of LVH include valvular heart disease, hypertrophic cardiomyopathy, dilated cardiomyopathy, ventricular septal defect, massive obesity, and amyloid heart disease. Among these, chronic severe valvular heart disease and hypertrophic cardiomyopathy are the most likely to result in severe LVH. In an examination of the hearts of 7,671 patients dying of various cardiovascular diseases, Roberts and Podolak (1985) showed that among the 23 patients with hearts weighing at least 1,000 g ("the King of Hearts"), 74% had aortic regurgitation either pure or associated with other valvular or congenital heart disease. The next most common etiology of massive cardiomegaly was hypertrophic cardiomyopathy (4 out of 23 cases).

Thus, in disease states, the limits of LVH are determined predominantly by the degree and duration of hemodynamic pressure and/or volume overload and any underlying genetic or hereditary susceptibility to cardiac hypertrophy.

LV Mass at the Limits of Physical Exercise

In contrast to the hypertrophy seen in disease states, LVH associated with extremes of physical exercise does not predispose to premature mortality. In fact, in a study of 235 exceptionally well-trained, multi-sport athletes, Douglas et al. (1997) found that most athletes had "normal appearing" hearts. LVH, defined using sex-specific criteria of 294 g in men and 198 g in women, was seen in only 17–22% of male athletes in comparison to 36–43% of female athletes. The importance of physical activity and cardiac work-load as a determinant of the limits of anatomic ventricular mass has been demonstrated in humans as well as several other species as shown in figure 2 (Holt et al. 1968). The concept of a "critical heart weight", proposed by Linzbach (1960, 1976) and Hort (1971) from their study of human hearts, suggests that an upper limit of 500 g for heart weight (reflecting a 75%–100% increase) may be seen as a result of exercise.

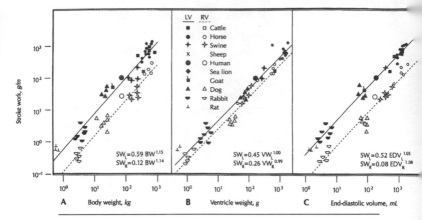

Figure 7-2. The importance of physical activity and cardiac stroke work as a determinant of the limits of ventricular mass has been demonstrated in humans as well as several other species (Reprinted from Holt et al. 1968; with permission)

Physiological Limits

The physiological determinants of LV hypertrophy fall under the two broad categories of mechanical and neurohormonal factors. As shown in Table 7-2, the mechanical parameters include elevated systolic and diastolic blood pressure, LV volume overload, arterial stiffness and increased LV myocardial wall stress. Among these, myocar-

TABLE 7-2: DETERMINANTS OF LEFT VENTRICULAR HYPERTROPHY

HEMODYNAMIC PARAMETERS	NEUROHORMONAL PARAMETERS
Increased Arterial Blood Pressure ↑ Casual resting systolic blood pressure ↑ 24 hour systolic blood pressure ↑ Ambulatory systolic blood pressure at work ↑ Systolic blood pressure at peak exercise	Increased Cardiac Sympathetic Activity ↑ Alpha-1 adrenergic activity ↑ Catecholamine levels
Increased Volume Load ↑ Obesity ↑ Dietary salt intake ↑ Cardiac output ↑ LV stroke volume ↑ LV stroke work	Activated Renin-Angiotensin System ↑ Circulating system ↑ Paracrine system ↑ Autocrine system
Structural and Functional Abnormalities of Resistance and Conduit Vessels ↑ Minimum vascular resistance ↑ Total peripheral vascular resistance ↑ Relative vascular wall thickness ↑ Absolute vascular wall thickness ↑ Vascular stiffness ↓ Vascular compliance	Effect of Growth Promoters ↑ Expression of growth factors ↑ Expression of proto-oncogenes ↑ Endothelin-1 ↑ B-type natriuretic peptide Intracellular Mediators of Hypertrophy • Diacylglycerol • Inositol phosphates • Calcium ions • Cyclic nucleotides
Increased Left Ventricular Wall Stress ↑ Peak systolic wall stress ↑ End-diastolic wall stress ↑ End-systolic and end-diastolic wall strain	

The strength of the evidence supporting a physiologically important role for these parameters varies. See text for discussion.

dial wall stress has been convincingly established as the principal stimulus for hypertrophy (Grant et al. 1965; Grossman et al. 1975; Strauer, 1979). The major non-mechanical determinants of LVH include cardiac sympathetic nervous system activity, renin-angiotensin system and growth factors. The complex relationships between these mechanical and non-mechanical factors are demon-

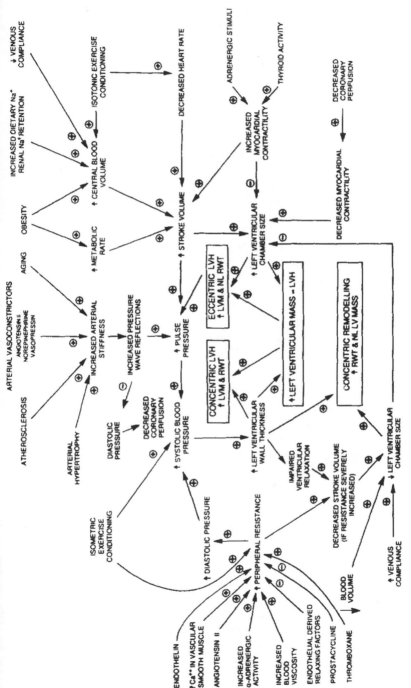

Figure 7-3. Hemodynamic stimuli in the development of left ventricular hypertrophy (Reprinted from Devereux and Roman, 1995; with permission)

strated in Figure 7-3. From a physiological point of view, the limit of LVH must be reached when a maximal myocardial wall stress is chronically applied in the setting of LV pressure and volume overload, increased cardiac adrenergic tone, exaggerated expression of growth promoters and a sustained activation of the renin-angiotensin-aldosterone axis. The strength of the evidence supporting a physiologically important role for the components of this theoretical construct varies as discussed below.

The principal stimulus for LVH is peak systolic wall stress which is importantly determined by systolic blood pressure, LV chamber radius and wall thickness. In spite of dominant role of systolic blood pressure in this relationship, casual clinic measurements of systolic pressure are only weakly correlated with LV mass. The extensive review of this subject by Devereux and Roman (1995) shows that (1) the weak correlation between systolic pressure and LV mass improves when 24-hour rather than casual blood pressure is considered; (2) daytime blood pressure level predicts LV mass better than measurements during sleep; (3) correlations between systolic pressure and LV mass are further improved with 24-hour measurements at work; and (4) the best correlation with LV mass is seen with exercise systolic blood (r=0.53–0.65 versus r=0.16–0.46 for casual systolic BP; Gosse et al. 1986; Ren et al. 1985; Nathwani et al. 1985). Compared to the systolic blood pressure, the level of diastolic blood pressure appears important in determining relative wall thickness rather than LV mass (Devereux et al. 1983A).

Left ventricular volume overload is also an important hemodynamic determinant of wall stress and thus, LVH. The imposed volume load leads to an acute increase in end-diastolic chamber radius (cavity enlargement) with initial decrease in wall thickness. According to the Laplace relationship, an increase in chamber radius and a decrease in wall thickness lead to increased wall stress even in the absence of an associated increase in blood pressure. The increase in wall stress stimulates an increase in LV wall thickness in order to normalize the wall stress. Appropriate compensation results in normalization of the wall thickness relative to the increased chamber radius, thus the development of eccentric hypertrophy (Ganau et al. 1992). Given this schema, it is not surprising that in both experimental and clinical hypertension as well as in control subjects, LV chamber size and stroke volume predict LV mass better than does systolic blood pressure (Ganau et al. 1990; Leenen & Tsoporis, 1990; de Simone et al. 1992 & 1993). This mechanism also appears important in the development of eccentric hypertrophy in the setting of obesity, increased dietary salt intake, chronic anemia, the physiologic hypertrophy of pregnancy and clinical high output states. Recent experimental data suggest that end-diastolic wall strain rather than stress may be the principal stimulus for development of LVH in the setting volume overload states (Emery and Owens, 1997).

Structural alterations in the resistance and conduit vessels that lead to an increase in vascular resistance and stiffness or a decrease in vascular compliance play a role in the development of ventricular hypertrophy (Schulte et al. 1993). However, significant relations of these parameters to LV mass and geometry have not always been consistently demonstrated (Lucarini et al. 1991). These inconsistent findings reflect the complex ventricular-vascular relationship and the relative contributions of peripheral vascular resistance and cardiac output to the maintenance of blood pressure. In addition, the role of non-hemodynamic factors appear important since LVH may actually precede vascular hypertrophy and the development of hypertension (Geri et al. 1985; Devereux, 1990; Post et al. 1994).

The important effect of these mechanical factors on LV chamber and myocardial wall stress and strain is well-established in the pathogenesis of LVH. However, several observations suggest that non-mechanical factors may be of equal importance in some cases. For example, non-pressor doses of catecholamines induce LVH (Alderman 1970; Laks et al. 1973); growth hormone and growth factors mediate the development of LVH (Lombardi et al. 1997; Donohue et al. 1997; Fazio et al. 1997); and angiotensin II mediates cardiac myocyte hypertrophy (Meggs et al. 1993) and may have an independent effect on LV mass in healthy young adults (Harrap et al. 1996).

Based on these and other studies, attention has been focused on cardiac sympathetic activity, renin-angiotensin aldosterone system and growth hormone as determinants of LVH. Consistent and definitive evidence is however lacking for physiological roles played by these factors independent of their hemodynamic effect. For example, in extreme clinical scenarios of hyperadrenergic states (such as pheochromocytoma) or hyper-reninemic states (such as high renin and renovascular hypertension), a primary effect of catecholamines or renin-angiotensin on LVH independent of blood pressure has not convincingly been demonstrated (Shub et al. 1986; Fouad-Tarazi et al. 1992; Vensel et al. 1986; Devereux et al. 1982).

From a physiological standpoint, the limits of cardiac hypertrophy must be reached when uncontrolled hemodynamic stress and strain from chronic pressure and/or volume overload persist in the setting of an activated neurohormonal milieu. Even in individuals without familial, hereditary or genetic predisposition to cardiac hypertrophy, these physiologic stimuli will lead to LVH.

GENETIC SUSCEPTIBILITY TO CARDIAC HYPERTROPHY AND BIOCHEMICAL MANIFESTATIONS

A genetic predisposition to cardiac hypertrophy, independent of mechanical or neurohormonal influences, is supported by several clinical and experimental observations. First, normotensive offspring of hypertensive parents have higher ventricular masses than control subjects with similar blood pressure (Nielsen 1985; Radice et al. 1986; deLeonardis et al. 1988). Second, values for LV mass are more similar in monozygotic than in dizygotic twins and this observation remains statistically significant after adjusting for level of physical activity, body size and blood pressure level (Fagard et al. 1987; Harshfield et al. 1988; Verhaaren et al. 1991). Third, Post et al. (1997) have shown that intraclass correlations for LV mass was statistically significant between first degree relatives (parent–child or siblings, r=0.15–0.16; p<0.001) but not in spouses or second degree relatives (r=0.05–0.06; p=NS). Fourth, a genetic susceptibility to cardiac hypertrophy independent of blood pressure has been demonstrated in inherited hypertension (Innes et al. 1998). These data provide convincing evidence of the importance of genetics and hereditary influence on LVH.

Recent advances in transgenic and gene-targeting methodologies as well as data from the available genome-based resources for cardiovascular medicine provide further evidence of the important role of genetic control of LVH. At the molecular genetic level, it is well established that mutation or overexpression of proto-oncogenes lead to hypertrophy or hyperplasia of cardiac cells (Starksen et al. 1986; Izumo et al. 1988; Jackson et al. 1990). In fact, Jackson et al (1990) showed that supranormal expression of the myc-gene led to a substantial increase in heart weight *in utero* and a 50% perinatal mortality. Like c-myc, the proto-oncogenes c-fos and c-ras appear important in the regulation of growth and the development of hypertrophy (Schneider & Olson, 1988; Mulvagh et al. 1988).

Hwang et al. (1997) have provided data on the analysis of gene expression in human cardiac hypertrophy. They have identified 48 genes that are potentially overexpressed in cardiac hypertrophy. Among these, the 23 genes considered "strong candidates for high expression" in cardiac hypertrophy included myosin light chain-2, brain natriuretic peptide, desmin, heat shock protein 70, and superoxide dismutase (Hwang et al. 1997). In addition to these, other genes identified in their study that have previously been shown to be elevated or involved in cardiac hypertrophy include atrial natriuretic factor, α-cardiac actin, β-actin and α-tropomyosin. The net result of the alterations in gene expression during hypertrophy is the increase in ribonucleic acid and subsequent protein biosynthesis. The increase in protein biosynthesis is both quantitatively and qualitatively heterogeneous (Swynghedauw, 1986). For example, in an experimental model of aortic constriction producing marked LVH and induction in the expression of β-MHC and atrial natriuretic factor genes, m-RNA for the former increased only 3.2-fold whereas it increased 10-fold for the latter (Hasegawa et al. 1997). Isoform shifts in the proteins synthesized, such as induction of "fetal" isoforms, further produce qualitative heterogeneity in the hypertrophic process. Further analysis of the roles played by alterations in gene expression may shed light on the quantitative and qualitative limits of LVH and the transition from normal function to heart failure in cardiac hypertrophy (Susic et al. 1996; Wakasaki et al. 1997; Hwang et al. 1997).

Molecular Mediators and Effectors of LVH

Although the exact mechanisms that transduce the inciting mechanical or neurohormonal stimuli to gene expression and protein biosynthesis is not completely understood, substantial amount of knowledge has recently accumulated regarding the molecular mediators and effectors of the hypertrophic process. The available evidence suggest that these molecular transducers include intracellular calcium ions, cyclic nucleotides, diacylglycerol and inositol phosphates. They are the common pathway linking the mechanical and neurohormonal stimuli to gene expression and eventual cardiac hypertrophy.

Clinical Relevance of LVH at the Limits

In discussing the clinical relevance of LVH at the limits, several important and practical questions need answering. Is there a threshold level of LV mass beyond which adverse events manifest? Can that threshold level be precisely identified in clinical practice? Which of the dozen or more criteria for LV mass partition values should be used to identify the limits of LVH? What are the clinical manifestations at the limits of LVH and are they independent of associated coronary artery disease, endothelial dysfunction and vascular remodelling? In the absence of hypertension or evident disease, should LVH or LV mass at the upper limits of normal be an indication for intervention? In this section, these questions as well as the overall clinical importance of LVH are discussed.

Although the precise mechanisms linking hemodynamic stimuli to the subsequent development of LVH are incompletely understood, there is now a wealth of data that provide compelling evidence of the clinical importance of LVH. It is now recognized and well established that ventricular hypertrophy has important consequences on cardiac systolic and diastolic function and most importantly, on cardiovascular morbidity and mortality. Data in patients with essential hypertension and members of the general population were the first to point out that LVH detected on the electrocardiogram was a powerful marker for congestive heart failure and cardiovascular mortality (Sokolow & Perloff, 1961; Breslin et al. 1966; Kannel et al. 1969; Kannel et al. 1972). More recent data have shown conclusively that other than age, LVH detected on echocardiography is a powerful predictor of fatal and non-fatal cardiovascular events and death from all causes (Casale et al. 1986; Aronow et al. 1988; Levy et al. 1989; Silberberg et al. 1989; Levy et al. 1990; Koren et al. 1991). Left ventricular hypertrophy was also more successful than the World Health Organization and blood pressure based criteria in predicting subsequent cardiovascular complications (Mensah et al. 1993). In fact, the data from the Framingham Heart Study showed that after accounting for conventional coronary risk factors, only age and LV mass index consistently predicted all three endpoints (cardiac death, all-causes death, and non-fatal coronary events) in both men and women in all age-groups (Levy et al. 1990).

While the studies cited above firmly establish the adverse prognostic value of LVH, they explain neither the basis nor the mechanism of attributable risk. Hypertension, the commonest cause of LVH, is also a powerful risk factor for coronary artery disease (Castelli, 1984; Stokes et al. 1989), the leading cause of cardiovascular morbidity and mortality. In addition, LVH is commonly seen in the setting of other co-existing target organ damage, including coronary and extracardiac atherosclerosis (Cohen et al. 1981; Roman et al. 1995). Increased levels of left ventricular mass index have also been shown to be more prevalent in patients with than without coronary artery disease (Cooper et al. 1990). Finally, LVH itself is an important marker of the presence and severity of coronary heart disease independent of conventional risk factors (Levy et al. 1989; Robinson et al. 1993). These observations led many investigators to question whether the risk seen in LVH was not mediated in whole or in large part through myocardial ischemia. The current consensus is that the strong prognostic ability of LVH detected by either ECG or echocardiography is independent of the presence or severity of coronary artery disease (Ghali et al. 1992; Sullivan et al. 1993; Liao et al. 1995; Mensah et al. 1995). This is true for adult male and female members of the general population, hypertensives and patients with other cardiovascular diseases.

For example, in our study of 1,089 black patients who had both echocardiography and coronary arteriography for evaluation of chest pain, we showed that the 5-year survival was lower in patients with LVH without significant CAD than in those with single vessel CAD (Liao et al. 1995). Most importantly, the 5-year survival was nearly identical in patients with LVH without CAD and those with multivessel CAD without LVH (Figure 7-4). In fact, the population attributable risk fraction was significantly higher for LVH than for single vessel CAD, multivessel CAD, and LV systolic dysfunction (ejection fraction < 45%). For every 100 deaths in our cohort, LVH accounted for 37 compared to 1, 22, and 9 deaths for single vessel CAD, multivessel CAD, and LV dysfunction, respectively (Liao et al. 1995).

Why is LVH so deleterious? The available experimental data provide some insight into the basis for the ominous implications of LVH especially in the setting of hypertension. LVH may sensitize the myocardium to ischemic

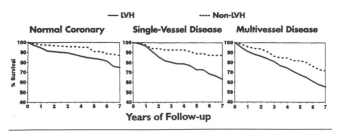

Figure 7-4. Survival in patients with and without left ventricular hypertrophy in the presence of no significant coronary artery disease, single vessel disease, and multivessel coronary artery disease. (Reprinted from Liao et al. 1995; with permission)

insults, increase the susceptibility to life-threatening ventricular arrhythmias and sudden death, impair diastolic relaxation and compliance, compromise coronary vasodilator reserve, and hasten the overall progression to eventual heart failure. First, the increased overall muscle mass of the left ventricle directly increases myocardial oxygen demand thereby sensitizing the myocardium to ischemic insults. Second, the increased muscle mass in LVH is rarely associated with a proportionate increase in the coronary microcirculation (Murray et al. 1981; Marcus et al. 1983). This lack of proportionate growth of muscle mass and coronary microcirculation produces an increase in diffusion distance for nutrients and oxygen thus predisposing the hypertrophied muscle to ischemia. Third, coronary flow reserve is impaired as a result of increased intramyocardial arteriolar resistance and abnormal endothelium-dependent vasodilation (Marcus et al. 1983; Treasure et al. 1993). Antony et al. (1993) have shown that impaired vasodilator reserve is not seen in treated hypertensive patients without LVH but is most marked in untreated patients with LVH. Fourth, abnormal coronary auto-regulation increased intraventricular compressive forces and mechanical compression from interstitial fibrosis may lead to additional impairment of coronary flow (Pearlman, 1982; Tanaka et al. 1987; Polese et al. 1991). Finally, increased interstitial fibrosis and collagen volume fraction often seen in LVH predispose to abnormal electrophysiologic properties, ventricular ectopy, life-threatening arrhythmia, myocardial and ventricular chamber stiffness leading to heart failure and sudden death in both human and animal studies (Aronson et al. 1981; Messerli et al. 1989; Pahor et al. 1991; Brilla et al. 1991; Ohsato et al. 1992; Vester et al. 1992). All these pathophysiologic mechanisms are worsened when there is coexistent epicardial coronary artery obstruction leading to further ischemia.

Is there a threshold value of LV mass beyond which these adverse effects are noted? Very much like the relationship between blood pressure level and hypertensive risk, the adverse events associated with LVH appear related to ventricular mass in a graded and continuous fashion. Thus, there is no clinically meaningful level of ventricular mass below which there is no risk and above which the adverse effects manifest. Increased LV mass index, defined as two standard deviations above the mean value in a healthy, normotensive population is a practical "threshold" for identifying increased risk. The higher the LV mass index, the greater the risk. Different sex-specific criteria and different methods for indexing LV mass to body size have been proposed. However, Koren et al. (1991) found that an LV mass/body surface area >125 g/m^2 identified fatal and non-fatal events in both men and women equally well and in the Framingham Heart Study, a level of LV mass/height >140 g/m identified high risk in both genders (Levy et al. 1990). In spite of these, there are over a dozen criteria for LVH using different methods of indexation for LV mass and different partition values for similar indexes in different study populations (Table 7-1). We compared the predictive value of echocardiographically-determined LVH on cardiac mortality and death from all causes using partition values for various methods of indexing LV mass (height, height^2, height$^{2.13}$, height$^{2.7}$, body surface area (BSA), BSA$^{1.5}$). All indexes of LV mass were very highly correlated therefore LVH defined by different indexes similarly conferred increased risk of mortality (Liao et al. 1997). However, patients with LVH defined concordantly by height-based and BSA indexes had the highest average LV mass indexes among all groups and experienced as much as a three-fold greater risk of death compared to those without LVH (Liao et al. 1997).

Regression of LVH

Given the weight of compelling evidence linking LVH to adverse prognosis, it would seem logical that regression of LVH would confer improved survival. There is at present no conclusive evidence that regression or reversal of established LVH improves survival. However, there are now at least five studies that suggest strongly that regression of LVH (detected by either electrocardiography or echocardiography) is safe and may improve survival. In Figure 7-5, a composite of the results from these regression studies is presented. Devereux's group (Koren et al. 1991) was the first to show that in patients with mild to moderate hypertension without complications at baseline, development or persistence of initial LVH was associated with a higher likelihood of morbid events compared to patients in whom LVH regressed or never developed (29% vs. 9% of patients, respectively). The prognosis was also worse in patients who had any increase in LV mass compared to those who had any decrease in LV mass (20% vs. 9%, respectively). Three additional studies used echocardiography to assess LVH at baseline and during follow-up (Yurenev et al. 1992; Muie-

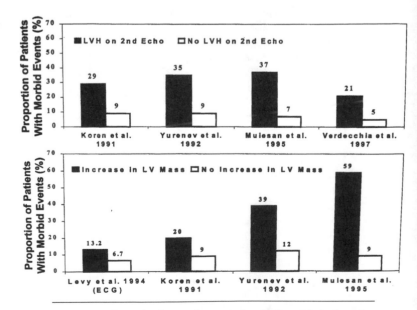

Figure 7-5. Composite data on the regression of left ventricular hypertrophy and morbid events in five clinical studies

san et al. 1995; Verdechia et al. 1997) and showed findings (consistent with the data of Koren et al.) that regression of LVH was beneficial (Figure 7-5). Levy et al. (1994) used the Cornell voltage criteria on ECG as a measure of LVH and assessed the incidence of cardiovascular events in up to 18 biennial follow-up periods in 524 participants of the Framingham Heart Study. An increase in Cornell voltage during follow-up was associated with nearly twice the likelihood of morbid events as in subjects who had a decrease in Cornell voltage. In a recent update of their hypertensive patients followed up for 1,217 patient-years, Verdecchia et al. (1998) showed in the 26% of patients with LV mass >125 g/m^2 at baseline, LVH regression detected on echocardiography was associated with a lower event rate than in those without regression (1.58 vs 6.27 events per 100 patient-years; p<0.002).

Devereux et al. (1996) reviewed seven electrocardiographic and ten echocardiographic studies with a total of 20,000 subjects and showed very consistent findings suggesting a greater risk of morbid events when LVH progresses (13–59%) than when it regresses (7–12%). Despite the consistency in the above LVH regression studies, a major persistent limitation is that none of the studies is randomized, controlled trials of sufficient sample size to provide conclusive evidence of the benefit of LVH regression. Thus, one must await data from current on-going large scale treatment trials and observational studies with an estimated 12,000 and 8,000 subjects, respectively (Devereux et al. 1996). Until these study results are available, however, it is fair to conclude from the available data that regression of LVH in hypertensive patients is safe and that all antihypertensive drug classes, including the older agents (diuretics and beta-blockers) but excluding the direct-acting vasodilators, can effectively induce LVH regression. Lifestyle interventions such as weight loss and salt restriction can also effectively cause LVH regression independent of blood pressure level (Himeno et al. 1996; Liebson et al. 1993).

FUTURE PERSPECTIVES

There are at least five areas in which the future holds substantial promise for improved patient care with regard to LVH. These areas include the definitive assessment of the benefits of LVH regression; improved understanding of the role of genetics and implications of gene expression in cardiac hypertrophy; genetic and pharmacological intervention for intentional induction of LVH; novel non-invasive imaging technology for improved ultrastructural and functional characterization in LVH; and a better understanding of the scientific basis for the transition from compensated hypertrophy to failure and excess cardiovascular morbidity and mortality.

First, the anticipated results from current on-going large scale treatment trials and observational studies with a combined patient enrollment of over 20,000 will provide definitive assessment of the benefits of LVH regression and whether specific drug classes have superiority over others in causing regression of LVH. Second, progress made in the Human Genome Project and the recent identification of the genes involved in cardiac hypertrophy provide another avenue for better comprehension of the regulation of hypertrophy and opportunities for intervention.

Third, intentional induction of LVH is another exciting field that holds future promise. The concept of LVH as an initially beneficial and desirable adaptation to conditions of chronic pressure or volume overload is well established but has not been adequately explored for therapeutic intervention. Several hormonal, procedural, and pharmacological agents have been used to induce cardiac hypertrophy in the setting of congenital heart disease, experimental heart failure, cardiomegaly and dilated cardiomyopathy. The most commonly used have been growth hormone, thyroxine, insulin-like growth factors, adrenergic agonists and surgically created hemodynamic pressure overload on the heart. For example, pulmonary artery banding, the first procedure in the two-stage arterial switch operation for transposition of the great arteries, has been the prototype of cardiac hypertrophy induced for therapeutic benefit (Yacoub et al. 1977) although several studies have shown an impaired LV systolic function in a proportion of patients receiving this procedure (reviewed in Wong et al. 1997). More recently, Wong et al. have shown that the administration of clenbuterol (a α_2-adrenergic receptor agonist) or thyroxine in conjunction with pressure overload induced a similar degree of cardiac hypertrophy without impaired systolic or diastolic function and unaccompanied by excess fibrosis compared to hypertrophy induced by banding alone. This seminal work from Wong et al. suggests that substantial degrees of cardiac hypertrophy can be induced without impaired systolic or diastolic function and may have clinical and physiologic implications.

Fourth, continued improvements in current imaging modalities for assessing heart size will be important (Mensah & Byrd, 1994). Novel approaches in diagnostic imaging technology that permit better assessment of the ultrastructural and functional changes in pathologic LVH also will be crucial in the clinical efforts at detection, evaluation and prevention of the transition from hypertrophy to failure. Finally, a better understanding of the scientific underpinnings that characterize the transition from compensated hypertrophy to cardiac failure is much needed.

Although there is much to be learned and gained from these future perspectives, a substantial amount of established fact exist to guide clinicians in patient management today. For example, guidelines for hypertension detection, evaluation and treatment now emphasize the prognostic role of LVH thereby appropriately influencing the urgency and intensity of blood pressure control in hypertensives with LVH (JNC VI, 1997). Similarly, the role of lifestyle intervention and all classes of antihypertensives (other than direct vasodilators) in reducing blood pressure and causing LVH regression without adverse effects is well established and should be emphasized in hypertension education.

Whether regression of LVH itself should be a goal of drug therapy must await results of the on-going trials.

SUMMARY AND CONCLUSIONS

Left ventricular hypertrophy is now well established as a powerful marker of adverse prognosis. Its ability to predict fatal and non-fatal cardiac events is seen in both men and women in the general population as well as in patients with hypertension and other cardiovascular diseases. Its relationship to cardiac events appears continuous and graded such that there is no threshold level above which events are present and below which adverse events are absent. The major determinants of the degree of hypertrophy are mechanical stimuli, neurohormonal activation, and hereditary and genetic influences.

In healthy individuals, the degree of hypertrophy is determined by body size, gender and extent of physical activity. Aging and blood pressure levels in the normal range have less impact on LVH. In disease states, the degree of hemodynamic pressure and/or volume overload determines the limits of LVH.

The ECG and echocardiogram provide the most practical approaches for clinical detection of LVH. Appropriate lifestyle changes and all antihypertensive drugs, with the possible exception of direct-acting vasodilators, can cause LVH regression. Progression or regression of LVH noted on, either ECG or echocardiography is associated with increased or decreased risk of cardiovascular events, respectively but conclusive evidence of this is not yet available.

REFERENCES

1. Abi-Samra F, Fouad RM, Tarazi RC. Determinants of left ventricular hypertrophy and function in hypertensive patients. *Am J Med* 1983; 75(suppl 3A):26–33. Ref

2. Adams TD, Yanowitz FG, Fisher AG, et al. Heritability of cardiac size:An echocardiographic and electrocardiographic study of monozygotic and dizygotic twins. *Circulation* 1985; 71:39–44.

3. Alderman EL, Harrison DC. Myocardial hypertrophy resulting from low dose isoproterenol administration in rats. *Proc Soc Exp Biol Med* 1970; 136:268–270.

4. Antony I, Nitenberg A, Foult JM, et al. Coronary vasodilator reserve in untreated and treated hypertensive patients with and without left ventricular hypertrophy. *J Am Coll Cardiol* 1993; 22:514–520.

5. Aronow WS, Epstein S, Koenigsberg M, et al. Usefulness of echocardiographic left ventricular hypertrophy, ventricular tachycardia and complex ventricular arrhythmias in predicting ventricular fibrillation or sudden cardiac death in elderly patients. *Am J Cardiol* 1988; 62:1124–1125.

6. Aronson RS. Afterpotentials and triggered activity in hypertrophied myocardium from rats with renal hypertension. *Circ Res* 1981; 48:720–727.

7. Bouthier JD, De Luca N, Safar ME, et al. Cardiac hypertrophy and arterial distensibility in essential hypertension. *Am Heart J* 1985; 109:1345–1352.

8. Bove KE, Rowland DT, Scott RC. Observations on the assessment of cardiac hypertrophy using a chamber partition technique. *Circulation* 1966; 33:558–568.

9. Breslin DJ, Gifford RW, Jr., Fairbairn JF, II. Essential hypertension:a twenty-year follow-up study. *Circulation* 1966; 33:87–97.

10. Brilla CG, Janicki JS, Weber KT. Impaired diastolic function and coronary reserve in genetic hypertension. Role of interstitial fibrosis and medial thickening of intramyocardial coronary arteries. *Circ Res* 1991; 69:107–115.

11. Casale PN, Devereux RB, Milner M, et al. Value of echocardiographic measurement of left ventricular mass in predicting cardiovascular morbid events in hypertensive men. *Ann Intern Med* 1986; 105:173–178.

12. Castelli WP. Epidemiology of coronary heart disease:the Framingham study. *Am J Med* 1984; 76:4–12.

13. Cohen A, Hagan AD, Watkins J, et al. Clinical correlates in hypertensive patients with left ventricular hypertrophy diagnosed with echocardiography. *Am J Cardiol* 1981; 47:335–341.

14. Cooper R, Ghali JK, Lancero L, et al. Prognostic significance of left ventricular hypertrophy after myocardial infarction:Divergent results based on electrocardiography and echocardiography. *Circulation* 1989; 80:II–46.

15. Cooper R. A note on the biologic concept of race and its application in epidemiologic research. *Am Heart J* 1984; 108:715–722.

16. Cooper RS, Liao Y, Rotimi C. Is hypertension more severe among U.S. blacks, or is severe hypertension more common? *Ann Epidemiol* 1996; 6:173–180.

17. Cooper RS, Simmons BE, Castaner A, et al. Left ventricular hypertrophy is associated with worse survival independent of ventricular function and number of coronary arteries severely narrowed. *Am J Cardiol* 1990; 65:441–445.

18. Dahlof B, Devereux R, de Faire U, et al. The Losartan Intervention For Endpoint reduction (LIFE) in Hypertension study:rationale, design, and methods. The LIFE Study Group. *Am J Hypertens* 1997; 10:705–713.

19. de Simone G, Daniels SR, Devereux RB, et al. Left ventricular mass and body size in normotensive children and adults:Assessment of allometric relations and impact of overweight. *J Am Coll Cardiol* 1992; 20:1251–1260.

20. de Simone G, Devereux RB, Camargo MJF, et al. In vivo left ventricular anatomy in rats with 2-kidney, 1-clip and 1-kidney, 1-clip renovascular hypertension. *J Hypertension* 1992; 10:725–732.

21. de Simone G, Devereux RB, Camargo MJF, et al. Influence of sodium intake on in vivo left ventricular anatomy in one-kidney one-clip and two-kidney one-clip Goldblatt rats. *Am J Physiol* 1993; 264:H2103–H2120.

22. deLeornardis V, De Scalzi M, Falchetti A, et al. Echocardiographic evaluation of children with and without family history of essential hypertension. *Am J Hypertens* 1988; 1:305–308.

23. Devereux RB, Agabiti-Rosei E, Dahlof B, et al. Regression of left ventricular hypertrophy as a surrogate end-point for morbid events in hypertension treatment trials. *J Hypertens* 1996; 14:S95–101.

24. Devereux RB, Casale PN, Hammond IW, et al. Echocardiographic detection of pressure-overload left ventricular hypertrophy:effect of criteria and patient population. *J Clin Hypertens* 1987; 3:66–78.

25. Devereux RB, Pickering TG, Harshfield GA, et al. Left ventricular hypertrophy in patients with hypertension:Importance of blood pressure responses to regularly recurring stress. *Circulation* 1983; 68:470–476. (1983A)

26. Devereux RB, Savage DD, Sachs I, et al. Relation of hemodynamic load to left ventricular hypertrophy and performance in hypertension. *Am J Cardiol* 1983; 51:171–176. (1983B)

27. Devereux RB, Lutas EM, Casale PN, et al. Standardization of M-mode echocardiographic left ventricular anatomic measurements. *J Am Coll Cardiol* 1984; 4:1222–1230.

28. Devereux RB, Roman MJ. Hypertensive cardiac hypertrophy:-Pathophysiologic and clinical characteristics. In:Laragh JH, Brenner BM. (eds). *Hypertension:Pathophysiology, Diagnosis and Management.* 2nd Edition, Raven Press; New York, 1995, 409 432

29. Devereux RB, Savage DD, Drayer JI, et al. Left ventricular hypertrophy and function in high, normal, and low-renin forms of essential hypertension. *Hypertension* 1982; 4:524–531.

30. Devereux RB. Does increased blood pressure cause left ventricular hypertrophy or vice versa? *Ann Intern Med* 1990; 112:157–159.

31. Donohue TJ, Dworkin LD, Ma J, et al. Antihypertensive agents that limit ventricular hypertrophy inhibit cardiac expression of insulin-like growth factor-I. *J Investig Med* 1997; 45:584–591.

32. Douglas PS, O'Toole ML, Katz SE, et al. Left ventricular hypertrophy in athletes. *Am J Cardiol* 1997; 80:1384–1388.

33. Eckner FAO, Brown BW, Davidson DL, et al. Dimensions of normal human hearts:after standard fixation by controlled pressure coronary perfusion. *Arch Pathol* 1969; 88:497–507.

34. Emery JL, Omens JH. Mechanical regulation of myocardial growth during volume-overload hypertrophy in the rat. *Am J Physiol* 1997; 273:H1198–204.

35. Fagard R, Van der Broeke C, Bielen E, et al. Maximum oxygen uptake and cardiac size and function in twins. *Am J Cardiol* 1987; 60:1362–1367.

36. Fazio S, Cittadini A, Sabatini D, et al. Growth hormone and heart performance. A novel mechanism of cardiac wall stress regulation in humans. *Eur Heart J* 1997; 18:340–347.

37. Fouad-Tarazi FM, Imamura M, Bravo EL, et al. Differences in left ventricular structural and functional changes between pheochromocytoma and essential hypertension. *Am J Hypertens* 1992; 5:134–140.

38. Ganau A, Devereux RB, Pickering TG, et al. Relation of left ventricular hemodynamic load and contractile performance to left ventricular mass in hypertension. *Circulation* 1990; 81:25–36.

39. Ganau A, Devereux RB, Roman MJ, et al. Patterns of left ventricular hypertrophy and geometric remodeling in essential hypertension. *J Am Coll Cardiol* 1992; 19:1550–1558.

40. Geri A, Agabiti-Rosei E, Muiesan ML, et al. Interrelations of cardiac and arterial vascular wall hypertrophy in essential hypertension. *J Hypertens* 1985; 3:s335–s337.

41. Ghali JK, Liao Y, Simmons B, et al. The prognostic role of left ventricular hypertrophy in patients with or without coronary artery disease. *Ann Intern Med* 1992; 117:831–836.

42. Gosse P, Campello G, Aouizerate E, et al. Left ventricular hypertrophy in hypertension:Correlation with rest, exercise and exercise and ambulatory systolic blood pressure. *J Hypertension* 1986; 4:S297–S299.

43. Grant C, Green DG, Bunnell IL. Left ventricular enlargement and hypertrophy. *Am J Med* 1965; 39:895–904.

44. Grossman W, Jones D, McLaurin LP. Wall stress and patterns of hypertrophy in the human left ventricle. *J Clin Invest* 1975; 56:56–64.

45. Grossman W, McLaurin LP. Diastolic properties of the left ventricle. *Ann Intern Med* 1976; 84:316–326.

46. Grossman W. Cardiac hypertrophy:Useful adaptation or pathologic process? *Am J Med* 1980; 69:576–584.

47. Hammond IW, Alderman MH, Devereux RB, Lutas EM, Laragh JH:Contrast in cardiac anatomy and function between black and white patients with hypertension. *J Natl Med Assoc* 1984; 76:247–255.

48. Hammond I, Devereux R, Alderman M, et al. The prevalence and correlates of echocardiographic left ventricular hypertrophy among employed patients with uncomplicated hypertension. *J Am Coll Cardiol* 1986; 7:639–650.

49. Harrap SB, Dominiczak AF, Fraser R, et al. Plasma angiotensin II, predisposition to hypertension, and left ventricular size in healthy young adults. *Circulation* 1996; 93:1148–1154.

50. Harshfield GA, Grim CE, Hwang C, et al. Genetic and environmental influences on echocardiographically determined left ventricular mass in black twins. *Am J Hypertens* 1990; 3:538–543.

51. Hasegawa K, Lee SJ, Jobe SM, et al. cis-Acting sequences that mediate induction of beta-myosin heavy chain gene expression during left ventricular hypertrophy due to aortic constriction. *Circulation* 1997; 96:3943–3953.

51A. Himeno E, Nishino K, Naskashima Y, et al. Weight reduction regresses left ventricular mass regardless of blood pressure level in obese subjects. *Am Heart J* 1996; 131:313–319.

52. Hodkinson I, Pomerance A, Hodkinson HM. Heart size in the elderly:aclinicopathologic study. *J R Soc Med* 1979; 72:13–16.

53. Holt JP, Rhode EA, Kines H. Ventricular volumes and body weight in mammals. *Am J Physiol* 1968; 215:704–715.

54. Hort W. Quantitative morphology and structural dynamics of the myocardium, functional morphology of the heart. In Bajusz E, Jasmin G (Editors). *Methods and achievements in experimental pathology*, vol 5, Karger:Basil, 1971.

55. Hwang DM, Dempsey AA, Wang RX, et al. A genome-based resource for molecular cardiovascular medicine:toward a compendium of cardiovascular genes. *Circulation* 1997; 96:4146–203.

56. Innes BA, McLaughlin MG, Kapuscinski MK, et al. Independent genetic susceptibility to cardiac hypertrophy in inherited hypertension. *Hypertension* 1998; 31:741–746.

57. Izumo S, Nadal-Ginard B, Mahdavi V. Proto-oncogene induction and reprogramming of cardiac gene expression produced by pressure overload. *Proc Natl Acad Sci USA* 1988; 85:339–343.

58. Jackson T, Allard MF, Sreenan CM, et al. The c-myc proto-oncogene regulates cardiac development in transgenic mice. *Mol Cell Biol* 1990; 10:3709–3716.

59. JNC VI. The sixth report of the Joint National Committee on prevention, detection, evaluation, and treatment of high blood pressure. *Arch Intern Med* 1997; 157:2413–2446.

60. Kannel WB, Castelli WP, McNamara PM, et al. Role of blood pressure in the development of congestive heart failure:The Framingham Study. *N Engl J Med* 1972; 287:781–787.

61. Kannel WB, Gordon T, Offutt D. Left ventricular hypertrophy by electrocardiogram. Prevalence, incidence, and mortality in the Framingham study. *Ann Intern Med* 1969; 71:89–105.

62. Koren MJ, Devereux RB, Casale PN, et al. Relation of left ventricular mass and geometry to morbidity and mortality in uncomplicated essential hypertension. *Ann Intern Med* 1991; 114:345–352.

63. Koren MJ, Mensah GA, Blake J, et al. Comparison of left ventricular mass and geometry in black and white patients with essential hypertension. *Am J Hypertens* 1993; 6:815–823.

64. Laks MM, Morady F, Swan HJC. Myocardial hypertrophy produced by chronic infusion of subhypertensive doses of norepinephrine in the dog. *Chest* 1973; 64:75–78.

65. Laufer E, Jennings GL, Korner PI, et al. Prevalence of cardiac structural and functional abnormalities in untreated primary hypertension. *Hypertension* 1989; 13:151–162.

65A. Lee DK, Marantz PR, Devereux RB, et al. Left ventricular hypertrophy in black and white hypertensives. Standard electrocardiographic criteria overestimate racial differences in prevalence. *JAMA* 1992; 267:3294–3299.

66. Leenen FH, Tsoporis J. Cardiac volume load as a determinant of the response of cardiac mass to antihypertensive therapy. *Eur Heart J* 1990; 11:s100–s106.

67. Levy D, Savage DD, Garrison RJ, et al. Echocardiographic criteria for left ventricular hypertrophy:the Framingham Heart Study. *Am J Cardiol* 1987; 59:956–960.

68. Levy D, Anderson KM, Savage DD, et al. Echocardiographically detected left ventricular hypertrophy:Prevalence and risk factors. The Framingham Heart Study. *Ann Intern Med* 1988; 108:7–13.

69. Levy D, Garrison RJ, Savage DD, et al. Left ventricular mass and incidence of coronary heart disease in an elderly cohort. The Framingham Heart Study. *Ann Intern Med* 1989; 110:101–107.

70. Levy D, Garrison RJ, Savage DD, et al. Prognostic implications of echocardiographically determined left ventricular mass in the Framingham Heart Study. *N Engl J Med* 1990; 322:1561–1566.

71. Levy D, Salomon M, D'Agostino RB, et al. Prognostic implications of baseline electrocardiographic features and their serial changes in subjects with left ventricular hypertrophy. *Circulation* 1994; 90:1786–1793.

72. Liao Y, Cooper RS, McGee DL, et al. The relative effects of left ventricular hypertrophy, coronary artery disease, and ventricular dysfunction on survival among black adults. *JAMA* 1995; 273:1592–1597.

73. Liao Y, Cooper RS, Durazo-Arvizu R, et al. Prediction of mortality risk by different methods of indexation for left ventricular mass. *J Am Coll Cardiol* 1997; 29:641–647.

74. Lie JT, Hammond PI. Pathology of the senescent heart:anatomic observations on 237 autopsy studies of patients 90 to 105 years old. *Mayo Clin Proc* 1988; 63:552–564.

75. Liebson PR, Grandits G, Prineas R, et al. Echocardiographic correlates of left ventricular structure among 844 mildly hypertensive

men and women in the Treatment of Mild Hypertension Study (TOMHS). *Circulation* 1993; 87:476–486.

76. Linzbach AJ. Heart failure from the point of view of quantitative anatomy. *Am J Cardiol* 1960; 5:370–382.

77. Linzbach AJ. Hypertrophy, hyperplasia and structural dilatation of the human heart. *Adv Cardiol* 1976; 18:1–14.

78. Lombardi G, Colao A, Cuocolo A, et al. Cardiological aspects of growth hormone and insulin-like growth factor-I. *J Pediatr Endocrinol Metab* 1997; 10:553–560.

79. Lucarini AR, Spessot M, Picano E, et al. Lack of correlation between cardiac mass and arteriolar structural changes in mild to moderate hypertension. *J Hypertension* 1991; 9:1187–1191.

80. Marcus ML, Koyanagi S, Harrison DG, et al. Abnormalities in the coronary circulation that occur as a consequence of cardiac hypertrophy. *Am J Med* 1983; 75:62–66.

81. Mayet J, Shahi M, Foale RA, et al. Racial differences in cardiac structure and function in essential hypertension. *Br Med J* 1994; 308:1011–1014.

82. Meggs LG, Coupet J, Huang H, et al. Regulation of angiotensin II receptors on ventricular myocytes after myocardial infarction in rats. *Circ Res* 1993; 72:1149–1162.

83. Mensah GA. Research issues and ethnic implications in essential hypertension. *J Assoc Acad Minor Phys* 1991; 2:168–173.

84. Mensah GA, Pappas TW, Koren MJ, et al. Comparison of classification of the severity of hypertension by blood pressure level and by World Health Organization criteria in the prediction of concurrent cardiac abnormalities and subsequent complications in essential hypertension. *J Hypertens* 1993; 11:1429–1440.

85. Mensah GA, Byrd BF, 3rd. Heart size:one-, two- and now three-dimensional echocardiography. *J Am Coll Cardiol* 1994; 24:514–516.

86. Mensah GA, Liao Y, Cooper RS. Left ventricular hypertrophy as a risk factor in patients with or without coronary artery disease. *Cardiovasc Risk Factors* 1995; 5:67–74.

87. Messerli F, Sundgaard-Riise K, Reisin E, et al. Dimorphic cardiac adaptation to obesity and arterial hypertension. *Ann Intern Med* 1983; 99:757–761.

88. Messerli FH, Nunez BD, Nunez MM, et al. Hypertension and sudden death. Disparate effects of calcium entry blocker and diuretic therapy on cardiac dysrhythmias. *Arch Intern Med* 1989; 149:1263–1267.

88A. Muiesan ML, Salvetti M, Rizzoni D, et al. Association of change in left ventricular mass with prognosis during long-term antihypertensive treatment. *J Hypertens* 1995; 13:1091–1095.

89. Mulvagh SL, Roberts R, Schneider MD. Cellular oncogenes in cardiovascular disease. *J Mol Cell Cardiol* 1988; 20:657–662.

90. Murray PA, Vatner SF. Reduction of maximal coronary vasodilator capacity in conscious dogs with severe right ventricular hypertrophy. *Circ Res* 1981; 48:25–33.

91. Nathwani D, Reeves RA, Marquez-Julio A, et al. Left ventricular hypertrophy in mild hypertension:correlation with exercise blood pressure. *Am Heart J* 1985; 109:386–387.

92. Nielsen JR, Oxhoj H. Echocardiographic variables in progeny of hypertensive and normotensive parents. *Acta Med Scand* 1985; 693:61–64.

93. Ohsato K, Shimizu M, Sugihara N, et al. Histopathological factors related to diastolic function in myocardial hypertrophy. *Jpn Circ J* 1992; 56:325–333.

94. Pahor M, Bernabei R, Sgadari A, et al. Enalapril prevents cardiac fibrosis and arrhythmias in hypertensive rats. *Hypertension* 1991; 18:148–157.

95. Pearlman ES, Weber KT, Janicki JS, et al. Muscle fiber orientation and connective tissue content in the hypertrophied human heart. *Lab Invest* 1982; 46:158–164.

96. Polese A, De Cesare N, Montorsi P, et al. Upward shift of the lower range of coronary flow autoregulation in hypertensive patients with hypertrophy of the left ventricle. *Circulation* 1991; 83:845–853.

97. Post W, Larson MG, Levy D. Impact of left ventricular structure on the incidence of hypertension. The Framingham Heart Study. *Circulation* 1994; 90:179.

98. Post WS, Larson MG, Myers RH, et al. Heritability of left ventricular mass:the Framingham Heart Study. *Hypertension* 1997; 30:1025–1028.

99. Radice M, Alli C, Avanzini F, et al. Left ventricular structure and function in normotensive adolescents with a genetic predisposition to hypertension. *Am Heart J* 1986; 111:115–120.

100. Ren J, Hakki A, Kotler MN, et al. Exercise systolic blood pressure:A powerful determinant of increased left ventricular mass in patients with hypertension. *J Am Coll Cardiol* 1985; 5:1224–1231.

101. Roberts AJ, Abel RM, Alonso DR, et al. Advantages of hypothermic potassium cardioplegia and superiority of continuous versus intermittent aortic cross-clamping. *J Thorac Cardiovasc Surg* 1980; 79:44–58.

102. Roberts WC, Podolak NJ. The king of hearts:Analysis of 23 patients with hearts weighing 1,000 grams or more. *Am J Cardiol* 1985; 55:485.

103. Robinson FC, Satterwhite K, Potter C, et al. Left ventricular mass index and coronary artery disease in hypertensive black males. *J Natl Med Assoc* 1993; 85:452–456.

104. Roman MJ, Pickering TG, Schwartz JE, et al. Association of carotid atherosclerosis and left ventricular hypertrophy. *J Am Coll Cardiol* 1995; 25:83–90.

105. Savage DD, Drayer JI, Henry WL, et al. Echocardiographic assessment of cardiac anatomy and function in hypertensive subjects. *Circulation* 1979; 59:623–632.

106. Savage DD, Garrision RJ, Kannel WB, et al. The spectrum of left ventricular hypertrophy in a general population sample:The Framingham Heart Study. *Circulation* 1987; 75:126.

107. Schneider MD, Olson EN. Control of myogenic differentiation by cellular oncogenes. *Mol Neurobiol* 1988; 2:1–39.

108. Schulte K-L, Liederwald K, Meyer Sabellek WA, et al. Relationships between ambulatory blood pressure, forearm vascular resistance, and left ventricular mass in hypertensive and normotensive subjects. *Am J Hypertens* 1993; 6:786–793.

109. Schunkert H, Jackson B, Tang SS, et al. Distribution and functional significance of cardiac angiotensin converting enzyme in hypertrophied rat hearts. *Circulation* 1993; 87:1328–1339.

110. Shapiro LM, Mackinnon J, Beevers DG. Echocardiographic features of malignant hypertension. *Br Heart J* 1981; 46:374–379.

111. Shub C, Cueto-Garcia L, Sheps SG, et al. Echocardiographic findings in pheochromocytoma. *Am J Cardiol* 1986; 57:971–975.

112. Silberberg JS, Barre PE, Prichard SS, et al. Impact of left ventricular hypertrophy on survival in end-state renal disease. *Kidney Int* 1989; 36:286–290.

113. Sokolow M, Perloff D. The prognosis of essential hypertension treated conservatively. *Circulation* 1961; 23:697–713.

114. Starksen NF, Simpson PC, Bishopric N, et al. Cardiac myocyte hypertrophy is associated with c-myc proto-oncogene expression. *Proc Natl Acad Sci USA* 1986; 83:8348–8350.

115. Stokes J, Kannel WB, Wolf PA, et al. Blood pressure as a risk factor for cardiovascular disease. The Framingham Study—30 years of follow-up. *Hypertension* 1989; 13:I13–I18.

116. Strauer BE. Myocardial oxygen consumption in chronic heart disease:role of wall stress, hypertrophy and coronary reserve. *Am J Cardiol* 1979; 44:730–740.

117. Sullivan JM, Vander Zwaag RV, el-Zeky F, et al. Left ventricular hypertrophy:effect on survival. *J Am Coll Cardiol* 1993; 22:508–513.

118. Susic D, Nunez E, Frohlich ED, et al. Angiotensin II increases left ventricular mass without affecting myosin isoform mRNAs. *Hypertension* 1996; 28:265–268.

119. Sutherland SE, Gazes PC, Keil JE, et al. Electrocardiographic abnormalities and 30-year mortality among white and black men of the Charleston Heart Study. *Circulation* 1993; 88:2685–2692.

120. Swynghedauw B. Changes in the genetic expression of membrane proteins as a determinant of myocardial dysfunction. *Acta Cardiol* 1996; 51:301–314.

121. Swynghedauw B. Developmental and functional adaptation of contractile proteins in cardiac and skeletal muscles. *Physiol Rev* 1986; 66:710–771.

122. Treasure CB, Klein JL, Vita JA, et al. Hypertension and left ventricular hypertrophy are associated with impaired endothelium-mediated relaxation in human coronary resistance vessels. *Circulation* 1993; 87:86–93.

123. Vensel LA, Devereux RB, Pickering TG, et al. Cardiac structure and function in renovascular hypertension produced by unilateral and bilateral renal artery stenosis. *Am J Cardiol* 1986; 58:575–582.

124. Verdecchia P, Schillaci G, Borgioni C, et al. Prognostic significance of serial changes in left ventricular mass in essential hypertension. *Circulation* 1998; 97:48–54.

125. Verdecchia P, Schillaci G, Borgioni C, et al. Prognostic significance of serial changes in left ventricular mass in essential hypertension. *Am J Hypertens* 1997; 10:25A (abstr)

126. Verdecchia P, Schillaci G, Borgioni C, et al. Prognostic value of a new electrocardiographic method for diagnosis of left ventricular hypertrophy in essential hypertension. *J Am Coll Cardiol* 1998; 31:383–390.

127. Verhaaren HA, Shieken RM, Mosteller M, et al. Bivariate genetic analysis of left ventricular mass and weight in pubertal twins (The Medical College of Virginia Twin Study). *Am J Cardiol* 1991; 68:661–668.

128. Vester EG, Kuhls S, Ochiulet-Vester J, et al. Electrophysiological and therapeutic implications of cardiac arrhythmias in hypertension. *Eur Heart J* 1992; 13 Suppl D:70–81.

129. Wakasaki H, Koya D, Schoen FJ, et al. Targeted overexpression of protein kinase C beta2 isoform in myocardium causes cardiomyopathy. *Proc Natl Acad Sci U S A* 1997; 94:9320–9325.

130. Wong K, Boheler KR, Petrou M, et al. Pharmacological modulation of pressure-overload cardiac hypertrophy:changes in ventricular function, extracellular matrix, and gene expression. *Circulation* 1997; 96:2239–2246.

131. Yacoub MH, Radley-Smith R, Maclaurin R. Two-stage operation for anatomical correction of transposition of the great arteries with intact interventricular septum. *Lancet* 1977; 1:1275–1278.

132. Yurenev AP, Dyakonova EG, Novikov ID, et al. Management of essential hypertension in patients with different degrees of left ventricular hypertrophy:multicenter trial. *Am J Hypertens* 1992; 5:s182–s189.

CHAPTER 8

Topical questions on the role of T and L type Ca channels in the heart

Denis Noble, Ming Lei, Hilary Brown, Prasad Ghapure, David Scollan and Raimond Winslow

INTRODUCTION

Interest in the roles of T- and L-type calcium channels in the heart, and elsewhere, has recently received a boost from the arrival of the first blocker, mibefradil, showing large selectivity for the T-type channels over the L-type channels. The result has been to re-open some questions that had been left to lie dormant. These include the role of T-type channels in pacemaker activity, and the influence of modulation of calcium channels on the ECG. These are the two questions I shall deal with in this article.

Ca CHANNELS AND SA NODE RHYTHM

Calcium channels play a major role in the generation of natural pacemaker activity in the heart (Irisawa, Brown and Giles, 1993). The most dramatic demonstration of this is the fact that the sino-atrial node region continues to beat even when the rest of the heart is arrested by blocking the fast sodium channels with tetrodotoxin. The upstroke of the action potential in the SA node is almost entirely dependent on L-type calcium channels, and these channels also play a role in the last third or so of the pacemaker depolarization when it reaches the foot of the activation curve for these channels.

By contrast, the functional role of T-type calcium channels has been less certain. On the one hand, nickel ions produce a significant (5-15%) slowing of SA node rhythm. If nickel is selective for $i_{Ca,T}$ this result suggests a moderate modulating role for these channels in pacemaker activity. It is therefore surprising that, when the kinetics of $i_{Ca,T}$ (Hagiwara et al, 1988) are incorporated into the single sinus cell model of the OXSOFT HEART program, the predicted time course of $i_{Ca,T}$ shows it to be exceedingly small, and to have a negligible contribution to pacemaker activity. The reason for this result is also obvious. The activation and inactivation curves in the results obtained by Hagiwara et al show so little overlap that, during the slow pacemaker depolarization, $i_{Ca,T}$ channels become fully inactivated before they have time to become activated.

This matter clearly needed re-investigation. There are several possible explanations for this inconsistency. First, it is conceivable that step voltage clamp results produce a poor basis for quantitative prediction of the current during more natural voltage changes such as the pacemaker depolarization. That would be true if the history of the voltage changes is important in determining the kinetic behaviour, for example if the rate coefficients for activation and deactivation did not depend uniquely on the instantaneous membrane potential. The second possibility is that the experimental results of Hagiwara et al have some systematic problem that led them to seriously underestimate the region of overlap between the activation and inactivation curves. Both questions have been tackled experimentally recently. The results obtained have also been used to re-compute the contribution of $i_{Ca,T}$ to pacemaker activity.

Results using combined ramp and step voltage clamp protocol

The first possibility can be tackled by using a different voltage clamp protocol from the standard step voltage pulses from constant holding potentials. The best protocol for this purpose is to impose the step clamps after first clamping the membrane to a ramp voltage change that closely mimics the pacemaker depolarization. Since the latter is, to a first approximation, a slowly rising ramp, this will produce a situation in which the subsequent steps will reveal the availability of the current following a history of potential changes similar to that of the pacemaker depolarization itself.

Lei, Brown and Noble (1995) performed such experiments in isolated single sinus node cells from the rabbit using a whole cell clamp via amphotericin-permeabilised patches. The initial ramp was imposed from a starting voltage of -65 mV with the ramp taking 75 msec to reach a voltage of -45 mV. Step voltage pulses of 125 ms duration were then applied to various voltages between -40 and $+20$ mV. The cells were treated with 30 μM TTX to block any sodium current, and 300 μM Nisoldipine to block L-type calcium current.

Figure 8-1A shows the results obtained. Clearly there is a significant transient inward current following each step depolarization. Figure 8-1B shows the relationship between the peak inward current and the membrane potential during the voltage clamp step. The maximum current is around -130 pA and the reversal potential is around $+20$ mV. The current inactivates rapidly within about 30 ms. The inward current is reversibly blocked by 40 μM nickel (not shown). These are characteristics consistent with the current being $i_{Ca,T}$.

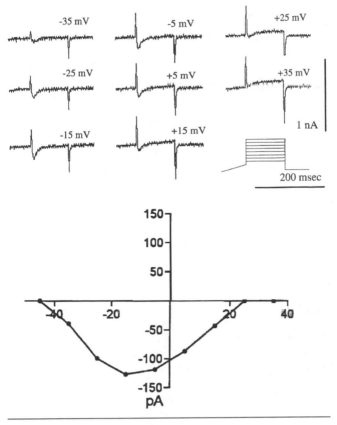

Figure 8-1 A: *$i_{Ca,T}$ was recorded in response to square depolarizing clamp pulses to the potentials indicated given after a 75 ms voltage clamp ramp rising at o.27 mV per ms from −65 to −45 mV, interpulse 500 ms. 30μM TTX and 300 nM nisoldipine present. Amphotericin permeabilised patch whole cell recording.* **B:** *I/V curve for $i_{Ca,T}$ from same cell.*

These results clearly establish that there is a significant availability of $i_{Ca,T}$ channels towards the end of the pacemaker depolarization. The channels are not therefore fully inactivated at this time.

STEADY STATE ACTIVATION AND INACTIVATION CURVES

The next question is whether this result is attributable to a failure of step voltage protocols to predict the results of ramp protocols or whether the voltage dependence of activation or inactivation is different from that estimated by Hagiwara et al. The steady state activation of $i_{Ca,T}$ was obtained by measuring the amplitude of inward currents during step depolarizations from a holding potential of −80 mV to test potentials ranging between −70 and +20 mV. The steady state inactivation curve was obtained using a double voltage pulse protocol with varying holding potentials followed by a test clamp to −40 mV. The results are plotted in Figure 8-2.

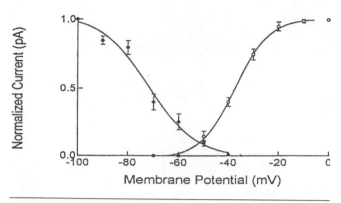

Figure 8-2: Activation- and inactivation-voltage relationships, dT and fT, for $i_{Ca,T}$ in SA node cells. dT was determined by voltage square pulses (inset) from the holding potential of -80 mV to various potentials and peak currents was normalized during the test potential to $+20$ mV ($i_{Ca,T}$/ $i_{Ca,T}$ max), fT was determined by using a double-pulse protocol (inset) and peak currents were normalized during test potential to -40 mV ($i_{Ca,T}$/ iCa Tmax). Averaged data were fitted by Boltzmann distribution equation and half-activation, half-inactivation potentials and slope factors were measured (see text).

The results obtained for the activation curve are fairly similar. However, those obtained for the inactivation curve are significantly different. We fitted the results with a Boltzmann distribution of the form:

$$a = 1/(1 + \exp([V_m - V_{\frac{1}{2}}]/k))$$

The half potential, $V_{\frac{1}{2}}$, in our results is -71 mV compared to -75 mV in those of Hagiwara et al. The largest difference however lies in the slope factor, k, which is 9 mV in our results compared to 6.1 mV in those of Hagiwara et al. The consequences of this difference are very significant indeed in precisely the range of potentials relevant to the pacemaker depolarization.

RECONSTRUCTIONS USING A COMPUTER MODEL OF THE SA NODE

This is best shown by using a computer model to demonstrate the consequences when the different activation and inactivation curves are used to compute the steady state current that would be expected to flow through the $i_{Ca,T}$ channels at various potentials. This has been done using the OXSOFT HEART program (version 4.6). Figure 8-3 (top) shows the activation and inactivation curves fitted by the program to the Hagiwara et al results and those obtained in Oxford. We also computed the steady state current that would be expected to flow through the $i_{Ca,T}$ channels. With the curves in the positions determined by Hagiwara et al, there is virtually no region of overlap, and the steady state current is negligible over the whole voltage range. In the steady state, therefore, as one moves in the depolarizing direction, the channels become fully inactivated before they

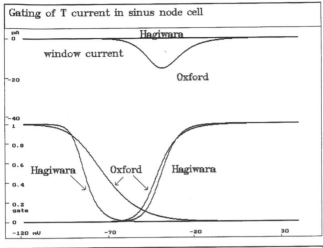

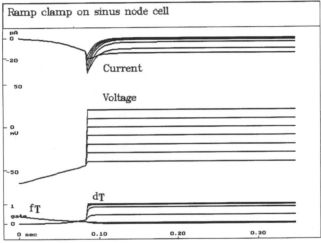

Figure 8-3. Top: activation and inactivation curves computed from the OXSOFT HEART program from the Hagiwara et al (1988) data and from the data obtained in the present paper. Bottom: Reconstruction of combined ramp-step voltage clamp protocol using the OXSOFT HEART program.

can be opened. Since the pacemaker depolarization shifts the voltage smoothly and relatively slowly, it is not surprising that computations of the contribution of $i_{Ca,T}$ to pacemaker activity using these activation and inactivation curves showed no contribution.

By contrast, with the curves fitted to the results reported by Lei, Brown and Noble (1995), there is very significant overlap between the activation and inactivation curves, with the consequence that a significant steady state current occurs in the pacemaker range.

Figure 8-3 (bottom) shows the results of using the computer program to mimic the combined ramp-step protocol used to obtain some of our experimental results. As the steps are applied at the end of the ramp, $i_{Ca,T}$ is clearly available and the amplitudes are similar to those recorded experimentally. This computation answers the second of the questions posed in my introduction. There is no need to assume that the history of membrane potentials makes a significant difference to the instantaneous kinetics of the channels in order to reconstruct the ramp-step protocol results since the computations simply use the activation and inactivation curves obtained in simple step clamp experiments. This is convenient since it makes computation of the role of $i_{Ca,T}$ in pacemaker activity easier than it might otherwise have been.

Figure 8-4 (right) shows a computation of sinus node pacemaker activity with and without the $i_{Ca,T}$ current included. The kinetics of $i_{Ca,T}$ were set to the experimental data obtained in the work of Noble et al (1998). The current generated by this channel clearly does have a significant effect on frequency. Removing the current from the model reduces the frequency by around 8%, which is very similar to the effect of nickel ions experimentally (Figure 8-4, left).

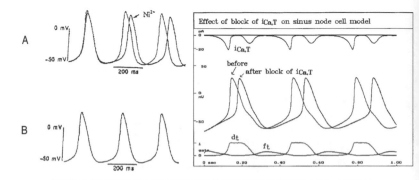

Figure 8-4. Left: *Effect of 40 μM NiCl$_2$ (to block $i_{Ca,T}$) on spontaneous activity of SA nodal cell. A, superimposed action potentials in control and after application of 40 μM Ni^{2+} for 5 minutes. The diastolic depolarization rate was decreased and cycle length was prolonged. B, after 5 minutes wash it gives nearly fully recovery.*
Right: *OXSOFT HEART model: computation of spontaneous activity in SA node cell model based on present results in the presence and absence of $i_{Ca,T}$.*

CONCLUSIONS CONCERNING SINUS NODE RHYTHM

The main conclusion is that $i_{Ca,T}$ channels do play a significant modulating role in natural pacemaker activity in the heart. Their presence increases the frequency by around 10%. A blocker of T-type channels would therefore be expected to produce moderate slowing of heart rate.

Figure 8-5 shows that in the conscious monkey this is the case. The R-R interval is clearly increased when mibefradil is administered.

A second conclusion is that this contribution of T-type Ca channels can be computed from the observed global kinetics of $i_{Ca,T}$ without assuming that step and ramp protocols have different effects on the instantaneous kinetics. We can therefore continue to use standard Hodgkin-Huxley type formulations for this current.

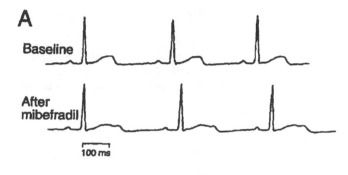

Figure 8-5. *Electrocardiograms recorded in conscious squirrel monkeys before (top) and after (bottom) administration of 30 mg/Kg mibefradil. Note the slowing of rhythm and that the T wave is flattened.*

ACTIONS OF CALCIUM CHANNEL BLOCKERS ON THE T-WAVE OF THE ELECTROCARDIOGRAM

Another issue of topical importance is the effects of calcium channel block on the electrocardiogram. Here we have recently encountered a major confusion, and it is time to clear it up. Those of us who teach cardiac electrophysiology to medical students may have to share some of the blame for the confusion. For, to simplify what to many is a difficult subject (not many medical students know the mathematics involved!) we often emphasise the relation between action potential duration and the R-T interval. Of course, there is such a relation, but it is important also to understand that the T-wave of the electrocardiogram is not simply a reflection of the time of repolarization; its form, amplitude and duration also reflect the gradients of activity in different parts of the heart. To understand the importance of this point it is sufficient to note that, were repolarization to occur simultaneously in all parts of the ventricle, there would be no T-wave at all! The T-wave, like all other components of the ECG is generated by differences in the waveforms in different parts of the heart.

This issue turns out to be of crucial importance in interpreting the effects of calcium channel blockers on the ECG. For, as the results shown in Figure 5 show that the action of mibefradil on the heart is not confined to block of T type Ca channels. In addition to the slowing of natural rhythm, there is also a very significant change in the form of the T-wave, which is flattened and broadened compared to the control situation. In fact a variety of changes in the form of the T-wave are observed at higher concentrations of mibefradil. The peak is always reduced. The overall wave is broadened and, in some cases, a distinct U wave appears. The latter effect may even appear to prolong the Q-T interval, which is puzzling since the main cellular action of mibefradil is to shorten action potential duration, as would be expected from partial block of L-type calcium channels. The paradox is further enhanced by the fact that careful analysis of Q-T intervals does not usually show a lengthening. The peak of the T-wave usually occurs slightly earlier.

We used whole ventricle computer modelling to answer the question whether action potential shortening would be expected to produce changes in the form of the T-wave that have hitherto been more usually associated with action potential lengthening.

WHOLE VENTRICLE COMPUTER MODEL

The model is based on a large-scale, biophysically detailed model of the canine ventricles incorporating known geometry, fibre orientation, and sheet organisation of the tissue (Hunter & Smaill, 1988; Nielson, LeGrice, Smaill & Hunter, 1991). The model is activated using a simplified description of the Purkinje conducting system (Durrer, Dam, Freud, Janse, Meijtler & Arzbaecher, 1970). The resulting electrical waves of depolarization are propagated through the heart, and ECG responses are computed by assuming the heart is immersed in a homogeneous volume conductor (Gharpure, 1996).

The action potential duration (APD) in different regions of the ventricles is set using the data of Franz, Bargheer, Rafflenbeul, Haverich & Lichtlen (1987) and Franz, Bargheer, Costard-Jackle, Miller & Lichtlen (1991). These investigators conducted a series of experiments in human patients in which they made a large number of MAP recordings on the endo- and epi-cardial surfaces of the heart in order to estimate cardiac APD as a function of activation time (AT). The result was that regardless of where on the epi or endo surfaces MAPs were measured, there was a simple linear relationship between APD and AT. These measurements have since been reproduced by Cowan, Hilton, Griffiths (1988). This APD(AT) relationship is referred to as the "Franz Function". Activation isochrones predicted using this whole heart model were tested against epicardial activation times obtained using a 240 electrode sock epicardial recording system in the dog heart (Gharpure, 1996). Model and experimental data agree well (unpublished data).

Winslow et al (personal communication) have used this model to investigate the effects of a large range of modifications of the Franz function on the ECG. The results show that simple linear manipulations of the Franz function, corresponding to uniform modification of action potential duration without change in shape of repolarization cannot reproduce the results of mibefradil. The linear manipulations do however show that small changes in APD produce large changes in T-wave amplitude and timing. This result suggests that small changes in the shape of repolarization may also produce large changes in T-wave form and amplitude. We therefore investigated the effects of allowing repolarization to start earlier, by reducing the 50% repolarization time while holding the 90% repolarization time constant. This change is illustrated in Figure 8-6. The resulting T-wave change is shown in Figure 8-7. It can be seen that

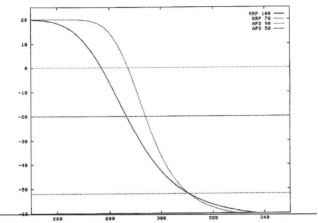

Figure 8-6. *This figure shows the change in repolarization waveform assumed to occur during the action of mibefradil. There is a 2% reduction in APD_{50} with no change in APD_{90}.*

this manipulation does succeed in reproducing the main features of the action of mibefradil: a substantial reduction of T-wave amplitude, a reduced time to peak and an increase in T-wave duration. It is noteworthy that, as with linear manipulations of the Franz function, small changes in action potential repolarization characteristics translate to large changes in T-wave form.

These results show that there is no incompatibility between a cellular action that produces earlier repolarization (as would be expected from block of L-type calcium channels) and a change in T-wave form of the kind found with mibefradil. Given the large sensitivity of the T-wave to even very small changes in repolarization characteristics, we can also conclude that when, as at therapeutic levels of mibefradil, the T-wave form is not affected, the changes in repolarization characteristics must be negligible. This is consistent with the fact that T type calcium channels are not

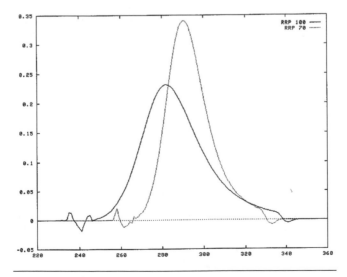

Figure 8-7. *Change in T wave computed before and after change in repolarization waveform.*

thought to make any significant contribution to action potential shape in the ventricle.

These results are clearly important. They show that action potential shortening, as well as action potential lengthening, can be responsible for flattening and broadening of the T-wave of the electrocardiogram. There is also a clear and rigorous test of this conclusion. If, in the case of mibefradil, these changes are attributable to L-type calcium channel block, then other L-type calcium channel blockers, such as verapamil, should produce similar changes in T-wave form. Figure 8-8 shows that this is indeed the case.

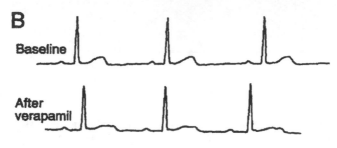

Figure 8-8. Recordings of ECGs in conscious squirrel monkey before and after administration of verapamil.

MULTI-COMPONENT T/U WAVE COMPLEXES

As noted previously, Mibefradil occasionally induces additional changes involving multiple components of the T-U complex. The most plausible interpretation of these changes is that U-wave amplitude is increased. An alternative, but less plausible explanation of these data is that in some fashion, the T-wave itself is decomposed into two separate components.

Winslow and his colleagues have investigated the effects of many different types of discontinuities of the Franz Function, each of which produce complex patterns of repolarization within the myocardium. All produce single peaked, large or small amplitude T-waves. None produce multi-component T-waves.

We may therefore conclude that it is unlikely that mibefradil contributes to the decomposition of the T-wave into multiple components. Rather, it is likely that mibefradil reduces T-wave amplitude, time to peak, and produces T-wave broadening by the cellular mechanisms described previously. These changes may in turn "unmask" the U-wave component.

This possible effect of mibefradil is illustrated in Figure 8-9. This figure is a schematic illustration of the dipole magnitudes (the lower amplitude curves) generated by repolarization at 6 different locations within the myocardium. One of these locations (dashed line) corresponds to the Purkinje/papillary tissue.

Figure 8-10 shows the effect of shortening recovery time in the ventricular region with no shortening of recovery time in the Purkinje/papillary tissue. This shift of ventricular repolarization results in the appearance of a new

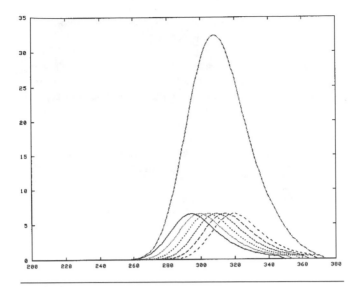

Figure 8-9. *Possible multipe-component T wave.*

peak generated by the Purkinje/papillary dipole. Indeed, the previous model analyses show that at high dosages, the action of mibefradil on ventricular tissue may produce a reduction in both T-wave amplitude and time to peak, as well as broadening of the T-wave. Multi-peaked T-waves would result if in addition mibefradil either delays or has little effect on Purkinje/papillary tissue repolarization. Therefore, temporal shifts required to produce multiple T-wave peaks could be produced by high doses of mibefradil if mibefradil has a differential effect on repolarization of the ventricular myocardium versus an anatomically distinct mass of tissue which is largely uncoupled electrically from the ventricular myocardium (for example, the Purkinje fibers and papillary muscles).

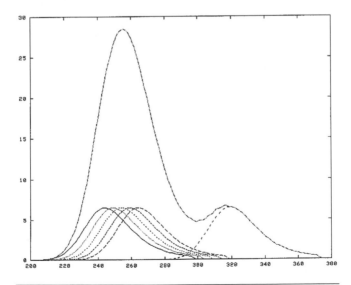

Figure 8-10. *Illustration of how shifting of all but one component to earlier peaks could reveal a U wave.*

CONCLUSIONS CONCERNING ACTIONS ON THE ECG

It is clear from these results that properties of the T-wave are extremely sensitive to small changes in spatial distribution of cardiac cell APD and action potential shape. Very small changes in cellular APD and/or shape produce significant changes in T-wave amplitude and time to peak without changing QRS interval. These changes in T-wave amplitude and timing occur in response to APD and shape changes so small that they are unlikely to be arrhythmogenic.

Conversely, since the T-wave is so highly sensitive to spatial distribution of APD and action potential shape within the heart, the absence of significant T-wave changes is strong evidence that the underlying patterns of cell APD and shape are largely unchanged. If changes in T-wave morphology are small, as in response to therapeutic levels of Mibefradil, then it follows that the underlying APD changes must indeed be negligible.

Small changes in T-wave morphology produced by therapeutic doses of mibefradil can occur in response to action potential changes that would not be expected to be arrhythmogenic.

Finally, the occasional emergence of multiple T-wave components following prolonged administration of mibefradil cannot be accounted for by any model which retains a smooth and continuous pattern of repolarization directed from either the epicardial to endocardial surfaces, or vice versa. Neither can this behavior be accounted for by models which incorporate simple discontinuities in the spatial distribution of APD and therefore repolarization time within the myocardium. It is more likely that multi-peaked T-waves result from differential effects of mibefradil on the repolarization of distinct anatomical regions of myocardial tissue which are relatively electrically uncoupled (ventricular tissue versus Purkinje/papillary tissue).

Acknowledgements: This work was supported by the MRC, BHF, Wellcome Trust and by Physiome Sciences Inc.

REFERENCES

Cowan JC, Hilton CJ, Griffiths CJ, et al. Sequence of epicardial repolarization and configuration of the T-wave. *Br. Heart J.* 1988; 60:424–433

Durrer D, Dam RTV, Freud GE, Janse MJ, Meijtler FL, Arzbaecher RC. Total excitation of the isolated human heart. *Circulation* 1970; 16:899–912.

Franz MR, Bargheer K, Rafflenbeul W, Haverich A, Lichtlen PR. Monophasic action potential mapping in human subjects with normal electrocardiograms: direct evidence for the genesis of the T-wave. *Circulation* 1987; 75:379–386.

Franz MR, Bargheer K, Costard-Jackle A, Miller DC, Lichtlen PR. Human ventricular repolarization and T-wave genesis. *Prog. Cardiovasc. Dis.* 1991; 33:369–384.

Gharpure PB. *A cellular automaton model of electrical wave propagation in cardiac muscle.* Department of Bioengineering. Salt Lake: The University of Utah, 1996.

Hagiwara N, Irisawa H and Kameyama M. (1988) contribution of two types of calcium currents to the pacemaker potentials of rabbit sino-atrial node cells. *J Physiol (Lond).* 395: 233–253.

Hunter PJ, Smaill BH. The analysis of cardiac function: A continuum approach. *Prog. Biophys. Molec. Biol.* 1988; 52:101–164.

Irisawa H, Brown HF and Giles W (1993) Cardiac pacemaking in the sinoatrial node. *Physiol Rev* 73: 197–227.

Lei, M, Brown, HF and Noble D (1995) Contribution of T-type calcium current to the pacemaker depolarization of rabbit isolated SA node cells. *J. Physiol,* 487P, 148–149P

Nielsen PMF, LeGrice IJ, Smaill BH, Hunter PJ. Mathematical model of geometry and fibrous structure of the heart. *Am. J. Physiol.* 1991; 260:H1365–H1378.

CHAPTER 9

Nitric Oxide: When will the limits be reached?

S Moncada, A Higgs and D Rees

The discovery that vascular endothelial cells produce nitric oxide (NO) from L-arginine (1) and that NO accounts for the biological actions of endothelium-derived relaxing factor (2–4) has led to many new insights into cardiovascular physiology and pathophysiology (for review see 5). The enzymes that generate NO (NO synthase) are present in a variety of cells of the cardiovascular system.

The synthesis of NO by a constitutive NO synthase in the vascular endothelium (eNOS) is a vasodilator mechanism which plays a role in the physiological regulation of blood flow and blood pressure in animals and man. Inhibition of the generation of NO by arginine analogues such as N^G-monomethyl-L-arginine (L-NMMA) leads to marked regional vasoconstriction and a hypertensive response (6). Mice in which the eNOS gene has been disrupted and which specifically lack eNOS have an elevated blood pressure compared with their wildtype counterparts (7). L-NMMA, which does not affect the blood pressure of the eNOS mutant animals, increases the blood pressure of wildtype animals to that of the mutants (manuscript in preparation, Figure 9-1).

The discovery of the NO-dependent vasodilator tone indicated the existence of an endogenous nitrovasodilator system, the actions of which are imitated by compounds such as glyceryl trinitrate and sodium nitroprusside (8,9). Nitric oxide also contributes to the control of platelet aggregation (10) and the regulation of cardiac contractility (11). These physiological effects of NO are all mediated by activation of the soluble guanylate cyclase. Other actions of NO that relate to the cardiovascular system include inhibition of white cell activation (12) and inhibition of smooth muscle cell proliferation (13).

Nitric oxide is now known to be the mediator released in the peripheral nervous system by a widespread network of nerves, previously recognized as nonadrenergic and noncholinergic (14–16). These nerves, which contain neuronal NO synthase (nNOS), mediate some forms of neurogenic vasodilatation but their role in the regulation of blood pressure has not been established.

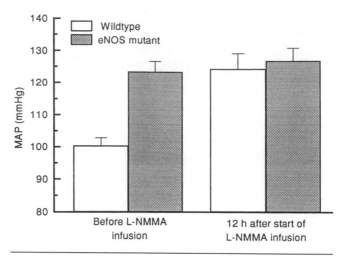

Figure 9-1. *Effect of L-NMMA on mean arterial blood pressure (MAP) in wildtype and eNOS mutant mice. Blood pressure, which was monitored continuously, was higher in conscious female eNOS mutant animals (n = 7) than in their wildtype counterparts (n = 8). Administration of the NO synthase inhibitor L-NMMA as a continuous infusion over 24 h (100 mgkg^{-1}h^{-1} i.v.) increased the blood pressure of the wildtype animals to that of the eNOS mutants (n = 5 for each).*

Impaired production of NO has been implicated in several cardiovascular disorders, including hypertension and atherosclerosis (for review see 5). One example of experimental hypertension in which there is unequivocal evidence for an impairment in the generation of NO is the Sabra hypertension-prone (salt-sensitive) rat (Figure 9-2). Compared to hypertension-resistant Sabra rats, vasorelaxant responses to acetylcholine are diminished in the hypertension-prone animals, the constrictor responses to L-NMMA are reduced, less eNOS is present in the vasculature, and the circulating levels of nitrite and nitrate (breakdown products of NO) are lower (17). Since NO plays a role in the excretion of sodium in the kidney (18) it is likely that a reduction in production of NO leads to a dual effect, namely an increase in vascular reactivity and reduced excretion of sodium, both of which play a role in the hypertensive state of these animals. Whether a decrease in production of NO in humans leads to similar pathophysiological mechanisms has not been established.

In rings of atherosclerotic coronary arteries as compared with rings of normal coronary arteries, the endothelium-dependent relaxation is decreased and the responses to vasoconstrictors are often enhanced (19). Furthermore, vasodilatation induced by increased blood flow or acetylcholine is impaired in the coronary circulation of patients with atherosclerosis (20), smokers and children with familial hypercholesterolemia (21). The administration of L-arginine normalizes this vascular dysfunction in patients and animals with hypercholesterolemia (22–24); in animals the effect is accompanied by a reduction in the thickness of the intimal lesions (24). Administration of L-arginine may be beneficial in preventing restenosis after balloon angioplasty, since it attenuates intimal hyperplasia in rabbits (25).

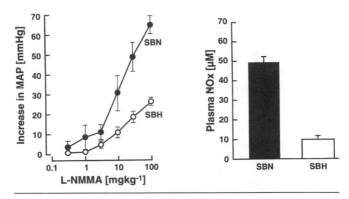

Figure 9-2. *Effect of L-NMMA on blood pressure and plasma nitrite/nitrate (NO_x) levels in the hypertension-prone (SBH) and hypertension-resistant Sabra rat. L-NMMA (1–100 mg.kg^{-1} i.v.) administered as a bolus over 30s elevated MAP in a dose-dependent manner to a greater extent in SBN than in SBH conscious rats (n = 3). The basal concentration of NO_x was significantly greater in SBN than in SBH rats (n = 4–5). These results suggest that the basal release of NO is lower in the SBH than in the SBN rat (see ref 17).*

Whether the effects of exogenously added arginine are due to its direct conversion into NO or to the fact that the added arginine may be promoting use of the endogenous substrate remains to be investigated. NO donors may also possess anti-atherosclerotic actions, based on the down-regulation of several processes involved in the progression of this condition. Thus, for example, the NO donor SPM-5185 markedly attenuates intimal thickening in injured carotid arteries of the rat (26). In this context it is interesting to note that eNOS knockout mice respond to vascular damage with a greater proliferative lesion than the wildtype controls (27).

Physiological generation of NO

The physiological generation of NO by eNOS is activated by a variety of chemical and physical stimuli. It may be possible to develop agonists that cause long-term activation of the L-arginine:NO pathway. Indeed angiotensin-converting enzyme (ACE) inhibitors, besides preventing the generation of angiotensin II, act indirectly in this way by preventing the breakdown of bradykinin, which stimulates the synthesis of NO (28). ACE inhibitors enhance the production of NO in endothelial cells (29) and treatment of animals with inhibitors of NO synthase reduces the antihypertensive effect of ACE inhibitors (28). The ability of these compounds to prevent formation of neointima after injury is also blocked by inhibitors of NO synthase, suggesting that these antiproliferative actions of ACE inhibitors may also be mediated, at least in part, via production of NO (30).

In some situations the activity as well as the amount of constitutive eNOS and nNOS is increased, showing that these isoforms of the enzyme can actually be induced. During pregnancy and treatment with oestrodiol mRNAs for both eNOS and nNOS are increased (31). This oestrogen-induced enhancement of NO synthesis could contribute to the decrease in vascular tone and contractility that occurs during pregnancy, the associated increase in gastrointestinal transit time and the reduced incidence of heart disease in pre-menopausal women. In addition, the induction of both eNOS mRNA and protein has been demonstrated following exposure of cultured vascular endothelial cells to shear stress (see 32). Shear stress-induced generation of NO accounts for the phenomenon of flow-mediated dilatation and might be a mechanism by which vessels keep shear forces constant in the face of changes in flow. Chronic exercise has also been shown to enhance eNOS gene expression in the aortic endothelium (see 32). These observations have led to the identification of consensus sites on the eNOS gene for regulation by shear stress and other stimuli (see 33).

Pathological role of NO

There is a different type of NO synthase which is inducible in many cells and tissues by immunological stimuli such as endotoxin lipopolysaccharide and cytokines and whose induction is inhibited by glucocorticoids (for reviews see 34, 35). This enzyme (iNOS) was originally identified in macrophages and contributes to the cytotoxic actions of these cells (36–38). The NO produced by this enzyme in the vasculature contributes to the profound vasodilatation of septic shock and may be involved in the myocardial damage that occurs in some inflammatory conditions of the heart (see 39). Endotoxin induces iNOS in the myocardium and endocardium and enhanced synthesis of NO by this enzyme may therefore contribute to the cardiac dysfunction associated with endotoxemia (see 40). Furthermore, the cardiac dysfunction of dilated cardiomyopathy is also associated with induction of this enzyme. Biopsies of myocardial tissue from patients with dilated cardiomyopathy have shown that this tissue contains iNOS whereas tissue from non-dilated ischaemic hearts or from patients with dilated hearts of ischaemic or valvular origin had little or no iNOS activity. The enzyme appears, therefore, to be expressed only in dilated hearts of inflammatory aetiology (see 40). Thus, in the heart as in the vasculature, NO may have a pathaphysiological role when generated by the constitutive enzyme that is normally present in the myocardium and may become pathologic, causing dilatation and tissue damage, when generated in large quantities and for long periods by the inducible enzyme.

One of the ways in which NO may be transformed from a physiological mediator to a pathophysiological entity may be through the actions it has on mitochondrial function. At low physiological concentrations NO inhibits cytochrome c oxidase in a reversible manner which is competitive with oxygen (41). At higher concentrations it irreversibly inhibits other enzymes in the respiratory cycle, either directly or through the interactions with superoxide anion leading to the generation of peroxynitrite (42).

L-NMMA, when used at low doses in animals and man, reverses the hypotension and the hyporeactivity to vasoconstriction characteristic of shock (see 39). Selective inhibitors of the inducible NO synthase may prove beneficial for the treatment of the hypotension of shock or cytokine therapy as well as provide a new approach to antiinflammatory therapy.

SUMMARY

The discovery of the L-arginine:NO pathway has changed our understanding of the physiological regulation of blood pressure, has led to the development of new models of hypertension and atherosclerosis and will ultimately lead to novel therapies for the treatment and prevention of cardiovascular disease.

REFERENCES

1. Palmer RMJ, Ashton DS, Moncada S. Vascular endothelial cells synthesize nitric oxide from L-arginine. *Nature* 1988; 333:664–666.

2. Palmer RMJ, Ferrige AG, Moncada S. Nitric oxide release accounts for the biological activity of endothelium-derived relaxing factor. *Nature (Lond)* 1987; 327:524–526.

3. Khan MT, Furchgott RF. Additional evidence that endothelium-derived relaxing factor is nitric oxide. In: Pharmacology, ed by MJ Rand and C Raper. *Elsevier, Amsterdam* 1987:341–344.

4. Ignarro LJ, Buga GM, Wood KS, Byrns RE, Chaudhuri G. Endothelium-derived relaxing factor produced and released from artery and vein is nitric oxide. *Proc Natl Acad Sci, USA* 1987; 84:9265–9269.

5. Moncada S, Higgs EA. The L-arginine-nitric oxide pathway. *N Engl J Med* 1993; 329:2002–2012.

6. Rees DD, Palmer RM, Moncada S. Role of endothelium-derived nitric oxide in the regulation of blood pressure. *Proc Natl Acad Sci, USA* 1989; 86:3375–3378.

7. Huang PL, Huang Z, Mashimo H, Bloch KD, Moskowitz MA, Bevan JA, Fishman MC. Hypertension in mice lacking the gene for endothelial nitric oxide synthase. *Nature* 1995; 377:239–242.

8. Moncada S, Palmer RMJ, Higgs EA. The discovery of nitric oxide as the endogenous nitrovasodilator. *Hypertension* 1988; 12:365–372.

9. Feelisch M, Stamler JS. Donors of nitrogen oxides. In: Feelisch M, Stamler JS eds. *Methods in Nitric Oxide Research.* John Wiley & Sons. 1996:71–115.

10. Radomski MW, Moncada S. Biological role of nitric oxide in platelet function. In: Moncada S, Higgs EA, Berrazueta JR, eds Clinical relevance of nitric oxide in the cardiovascular system. *Madrid: EDICOMPLET* 1991:45–56.

11. Kelly RA, Balligand J-L, Smith TW. Nitric oxide and cardiac function. *Circ Res* 1996; 79:363–380.

12. Kubes P, Suzuki M, Granger DN. Nitric oxide: an endogenous modulator of leukocyte adhesion. *Proc Natl Acad Sci, USA* 1991; 88:4651–4655.

13. Garg UC, Hassid A. Nitric oxide-generating vasodilators and 8-bromo-cyclic guanosine monophosphate inhibit mitogenesis and

proliferation of cultured rat vascular smooth muscle cells. *J Clin Invest* 1989; 83:1774–1777.

14. Gillespie JS, Liu X, Martin W. The neurotransmitter of the non-adrenergic non-cholinergic inhibitory nerves to smooth muscle of the genital system. In: Nitric Oxide from L-arginine: A Bioregulatory System, ed by S Moncada and EA Higgs. *Elsevier Science Publishers BV Amsterdam* 1990:147–164.

15. Rand MJ. Nitrergic transmission: nitric oxide as a mediator of non-adrenergic, non-cholinergic neuro-effector transmission. *Clin Exp Pharmacol Physiol* 1992; 19:147–169.

16. Toda N. Nitric oxide and the regulation of cerebral arterial tone. In: Nitric oxide in the nervous system, ed by S Vincent. *Academic Press Ltd, Orlando* 1995:207–225.

17. Rees D, Ben-Ishay D, Moncada S. Nitric oxide and the regulation of blood pressure in the hypertension-prone and hypertension-resistant Sabra rat. *Hypertension* 1996; 28:367–371.

18. Lahera V, Salom MG, Miranda-Guardiola F, Moncada S, Romero JC. Effects of N^G-nitro-L-arginine methyl ester on renal function and blood pressure. *Am J Physiol* 1991; 261:F1033–F1037.

19. Forstermann U. Properties and mechanisms of production and action of endothelium-derived relaxing factor. *J Cardiovasc Pharmacol* 1986; 8:S45–S51.

20. Cox DA, Vita JA, Treasure CB et al. Atherosclerosis impairs flow-mediated dilation of coronary arteries in humans. *Circulation* 1989; 80:458–465.

21. Celermajer DS, Sorensen KE, Gooch VM et al. Non-invasive detection of endothelial dysfunction in children and adults at risk of atherosclerosis. *Lancet* 1992; 340:1111–1115.

22. Drexler H, Zeiher AM, Meinzer K, Just H. Correction of endothelial dysfunction in coronary microcirculation of hypercholesterolaemic patients by L-arginine. *Lancet* 1991; 338:1546–1550.

23. Creager MA, Gallagher SJ, Girerd XJ, Coleman SM, Dzau VJ, Cooke JP. L-arginine improves endothelium-dependent vasodilation in hypercholesterolaemic humans. *J Clin Invest* 1992; 90:1248–1253.

24. Cooke JP, Tsao P. Cellular mechanisms of atherogenesis and the effects of nitric oxide. *Curr Opin Cardiol* 1992; 7:799–804.

25. McNamara DB, Bedi B, Aurora H, Tena L, Ignarro LJ, Kadowitz PJ, Akers DL. L-arginine inhibits balloon catheter-induced intimal hyperplasia. *Biochem Biophys Res Commun* 1993; 193:291–296.

26. Lefer AM, Lefer DJ. Therapeutic role of nitric oxide donors in the treatment of cardiovascular disease. *Drugs of the Future* 1994; 19:665–672.

27. Moroi M, Zhang L, Yasuda T, Virmani R, Gold HK, Fishman MC, Huang PL. Interaction of genetic deficiency of endothelial nitric oxide, gender and pregnancy in vascular response to injury in mice. *J Clin Invest* 1998; 101:1225–1232.

28. Cachofeiro V, Sakakibara T, Nasijletti A. Kinins, nitric oxide and the hypotensive effect of captopril and ramiprilat in hypertension. *Hypertension* 1992; 19:138–145.

29. Grafe M, Bossaller C, Graf K, Auch-Schwelk W, Baumgarten CR, Hildebrandt A, Fleck E. Effect of angiotensin-converting-enzyme inhibition on bradykinin metabolism by vascular endothelial cells. *Am J Physiol* 1993; 264:H1493–H1497.

30. Farhy RD, Carretero OA, Ho KL, Scicli AG. Role of kinins and nitric oxide in the effects of angiotensin-converting-enzyme inhibitors on neointima formation. *Cir Res* 1993; 72:1202–1210.

31. Weiner CP, Lizasoain I, Baylis SA, Knowles RG, Charles IG, Moncada S. Induction of calcium-dependent nitric oxide synthases by sex hormones. *Proc Natl Acad Sci, USA* 1994; 91:5212–5216.

32. Sessa WC. The nitric oxide synthase family of proteins. *J Vasc Res* 1994; 31:131–143.

33. Nathan C, Xie QW. Regulation of biosynthesis of nitric oxide. *J Biol Chem* 1994; 269:13725–13728.

34. Nathan CF, Hibbs JB Jr. Role of nitric oxide synthesis in macrophage antimicrobial activity. *Curr Opin Immunol* 1991; 3:65–70.

35. Nussler AK, Billiar TR. Inflammation, immunoregulation and inducible nitric oxide synthase. *J Leukoc Biol* 1993; 54:171–178.

36. Hibbs JB Jr, Taintor RR, Vavrin Z, Rachlin EM. Nitric oxide: a cytotoxic activated macrophage effector molecule. *Biochem Biophys Res Commun* 1998; 157:87–94.

37. Marletta MA, Yoon PS, Iyengar R, Leaf CD, Wishnok JS. Macrophage oxidation of L-arginine to nitrite and nitrate: nitric oxide is an intermediate. *Biochemistry* 1988; 27:8706–8711.

38 . Stuehr D, Gross S, Sakuma I, Levi R, Nathan C. Activated murine macrophages secrete a metabolite of arginine with the bioactivity of endothelium-derived relaxing factor and the chemical reactivity of nitric oxide. *J Exp Med* 1989; 169:1011–1020.

39. Vallance P, Moncada S. Role of endogenous nitric oxide in septic shock. *New Horizons* 1993; 1:77–87.

40. de Belder A, Moncada S. Cardiomyopathy: a role for nitric oxide? *Int J Cardiol* 1995; 50:263–268.

41. Cleeter MWJ, Cooper JM, Darley-Usmar VM, Moncada S, Schapira AHV. Reversible inhibition of cytochrome c oxidase, the terminal enzyme of the mitochondrial respiratory chain, by nitric oxide. *FEBS Letts* 1994; 345:50–54.

42. Lizasoain I, Moro MA, Knowles RG, Darley-Usmar V, Moncada S. Nitric oxide and peroxynitrite exert distinct effects on mitochondrial respiration which are differentially blocked by glutathione or glucose. *Biochem J* 1996; 314:877–880.